WRITING YOUR COLLEGE ADMISSIONS ESSAY

BY GERALD NEWMAN AND
ELEANOR WEINTRAUB NEWMAN

WRITING YOUR COLLEGE ADMISSIONS ESSAY

A GROLIER COMPANY

FRANKLIN WATTS
NEW YORK | LONDON | TORONTO | SYDNEY | 1987
A LANGUAGE POWER BOOK

378
NEW

Frontis: Driscoll University Center Bridge,
University of Denver, Colorado

Photographs courtesy of: Texas Christian University:
p. 2; University of Puget Sound: p. 12; Earlham
College: p. 38 (Tom Strickland); Monkmeyer Press:
pp. 60 (Mimi Forsyth), 90 (Michael Kagan); Davidson
College: p. 74; University of Denver: p. 124.

Library of Congress Cataloging-in-Publication Data

Newman, Gerald.
Writing your college admissions essay.

(A Language power book)
Includes index.
Summary: A guide to organizing, writing, and
revising essays for college admission applications,
with tips on being informative, personal, and
original. Also discusses sample answers to
typical questions and includes essays written by
students in actual college applications.
1. College applications—United States. 2. Exposi-
tion (Rhetoric) 3. Universities and colleges—
United States—Admission. [1. College applications.
2. Universities and colleges—Admissions] I. Newman,
Eleanor Weintraub. II. Title. III. Series.
LB2351.52.U6N48   1987   378'.1056   87-10411
ISBN 0-531-10428-1

CONTENTS

THIS BOOK IS DEDICATED WITH LOVE TO
AARON ROY NEWMAN,
WHO INSPIRES EVERYTHING WE DO.

ACKNOWLEDGMENTS

The authors extend their gratitude to the following contributors:

Shirley Bloomquist
Mona Bregman
Maria Buccellato
Marietta Cosentino
Joshua Frank
Andrew Fried
Sharon Gibson
Rochelle Granville, Ed.D.

Zulfiqar Malik
John Rehfeldt
Cheri Rosen
David Samuels
Debbie Samuels
Rebecca Samuels
Harris Sarney
Aimee Su

And to these directors of admissions for their valuable advice:

Henry F. Bedford, Amherst College
Michael C. Behnke, Massachusetts Institute of Technology
Richard W. Haines, Lafayette College
Stirling L. Huntley, California Institute of Technology
Nancy Hargrave Meislahn, Cornell University
Phillip F. Smith, Williams College
Richard Steele, Duke University

He who has hit upon a subject suited
to his powers will never fail to find
eloquent words and lucid arrangement.

—Horace, c. 8 B.C.

INTRODUCTION

Applying to college is a ritual that has always been associated with varying degrees of stress, worry, bickering, competitiveness, agony, ecstasy, jealousy, and a host of other behavioral responses from which you, your friends, and your family are probably not immune.

For most of you, the selection of a college is the first important decision you will make. Clearly, there will be influences upon your decision over which you may have no control: the fact that your scholastic record is almost complete, that your SATs/ACTs have been taken, and your family's financial ability to support your choice all weigh into your decision. But let's just put these considerations aside for a moment.

There are other influences over which you *do* have control. First and most important is that your choice should be one that will make *you* happy, not your parents happy or your friends green with envy. It's you who have to spend years of your life at whatever institution you select. Therefore, it is not unreasonable to screen out those influences that could result in your entrance into a college you might absolutely abhor. You haven't spent seventeen or eighteen years of your life learning to be dependent upon others. You're old enough to depend on your own instincts (over which, incidentally, your family and friends have exerted their influence). And, if you are honest with yourself, your instincts will very seldom be incorrect.

Your objective is to make your selection as pressure-free as possible. You can do it, too, because your graduating class demographically exemplifies the one age group in the U.S. Census Bureau population projection that shows negative growth. From 1985 to 1990, it was projected, your age group will exhibit no growth. In fact, the population will have dropped by 7.9 percent. By 1995, your age group will have exhibited 0 percent of growth. The implications are very positive for you.

In the baby-boom generation, which preceded you, the competition for seats at higher-education institutions, especially the Ivies, became excruciating. Well, baby-boomers have aged, and today almost every college wants students and their money more than they did before. Those empty seats formerly filled by baby-boomers have to be occupied by someone, or the school will lose out.

If that information doesn't comfort you, then take a look at how the colleges are romancing you. Fifteen years ago colleges weren't advertising on television, using direct-mail solicitations, spending thousands of dollars on brochures, and purchasing lists from the College Entrance Examination Board (CEEB) of names of potential entrants based on College Board scores; now they do. Many colleges are willing to spend over $1,000 per freshman recruited. And, according to *Madison Avenue Magazine*, average college recruitment budgets topped $700,000 in 1984 alone. Does this suggest to you that the chances of success are in your favor now?

By understanding and reminding yourself that most colleges want you more than you may want them, you've gained a modicum of control you thought you didn't have. But don't go off cocky in a belief that they're all just waiting for your nod. Colleges haven't lost their minds completely. They certainly do maintain standards.

Therefore, the next avenue over which you may gain control is in meeting these standards. Although your grades, boards, and extracurricular activities speak for themselves, the interview and, more important, the essay portion of the application allow you to speak for yourself. In fact, the college admissions essay has been cited by many admissions officers as that part of the application that may set you apart from your peers. This book is written specifically as an aid to writing the various types of college admissions essays.

You've written essays before, but now the stakes are much higher than just getting an A in English composition. This particular essay, by its very nature, is like none other. It will allow you the chance to express your ideas in a new way.

Written expression, as you know, is at first a discipline, and when practiced enough, it becomes an art. It is a skill that will serve you well right now, as you begin your quest for higher education, and as you continue into the future.

This book will prepare you to write your very best. It will also help you to understand that the parallels between the processes involved in writing an outstanding essay, such as

- understanding the options
- organizing the thought content
- stylizing to express your point of view
- and completing the task to your satisfaction

are the same processes that can be applied in all decision-making.

Now let's begin.

Jones Hall, University of Puget Sound, Washington

GETTING
STARTED

1

WRITING TO THE COLLEGES

It's impractical and rather expensive to apply to dozens of schools. But you'll need to know more about the colleges you are considering before applying. The best way to learn is to send a postcard to the schools that interest you. It isn't necessary to send a formal letter. Besides, it's easier for the Admissions Office to sift through cards than to open letters. A paragraph similar to the one below, clearly written or typed, is all you need:

> To the Admissions Office:
>
> I am a senior at Kennedy High School and am interested in attending Stanford University. Please send me your admittance application, the school bulletin, and any other information about Stanford that may be helpful. Thank you.

If you are typing, sign your name above your typed name and address. Address the card to the Admissions Office of the colleges you choose. Their proper addresses can be found in any of the popular college guides (Barrons, Lovejoy, Peterson, etc.). You will notice that most colleges do not have street addresses, so be sure to include the zip code.

THE BUSINESS LETTER

At a later date, you may want to write to the admissions officers of the schools that definitely interest you.

Remember that every bit of writing you submit to a college becomes a source of information for the college. Therefore, even a letter of request should be well written.

If you are uncertain of the correct form of a business letter, consult your grammar or writing textbook, where you will find detailed information about proper letter construction and samples of business letters. Though not the only way to write a business letter, one method after which you may pattern yours is as follows:

Heading —

210 Wellington Avenue
Auburn, CA 95603
December 28, 1987

Inside —
Address

Mr. John Bunnell
Director of Freshman Admissions
Office of Undergraduate Admissions
Old Union, Stanford University
Stanford, CA 94305

Salutation — Dear Mr. Bunnell:

Body —

I am a senior at Kennedy High School and have applied to Stanford University for admission in September 1988. In order to learn as much as possible about Stanford, I would like to visit your campus. Would it be possible for me to attend a few classes and spend a night in one of the dormitories?

Because Kennedy High School will be closed then, the best day for me to visit your campus is Friday, February 12, 1988. Please let me know at your earliest convenience if you can accommodate me on that date.

Closing ———————————— Very truly yours,

Susan B. Anthony

Signature ———————————— Susan B. Anthony

Heading

If you have your own business-size or personalized, self-addressed stationery, you need not type a heading. You need only include the date, typed about an inch down from the letterhead. It should begin at the center of the page.

Inside address

Skip a line and write or type the recipient's address at the left margin. The name of the person to whom you are writing should be included. It is far more courteous to send your letter to Mr. John Bunnell, Director of Freshman Admissions, than merely to an elusive Office of Undergraduate Admissions. Be sure to include Mr., Miss, Mrs., or Ms. as the college guide you are using lists it, and be certain you have spelled the person's name correctly. A good first impression can be marred by misspelling the name. After all, this is a person whose decision may affect the rest of your life.

The admissions officer's title may follow the name, or may be written (or typed) below it if the line will be unusually long. If the title follows the name, place a comma after the name. If you begin a new line for the title, do not place a comma at the end of the officer's name.

Mr. Henry F. Bedford
Dean of Admissions
Amherst College
Amherst, MA 01022

Mr. John Bunnell
Director of Freshman Admissions
Office of Undergraduate Admissions
Old Union, Stanford University
Stanford, CA 94305

Salutation
Address the school's admissions officer by name. It's the courteous thing to do. After skipping a line under the inside address, at the margin write:

Dear Dean (or Mr., Miss, Mrs., Ms.) __:

To avoid writing in a vacuum, never begin a letter with "To whom it may concern:". Such a greeting lacks personal contact. A colon follows the greeting.

Body
To begin the body of your letter, skip a line under the salutation and indent as you would when writing any paragraph.

Your letter should briefly and courteously discuss your immediate concern, such as visiting the school or asking specific questions, whose answers cannot be found in the college catalog. This is not the time to ask personal questions or to make any comments.

Closing
Skip a line, then write or type the closing, aligning it with the date. A few proper closings are: "Very truly yours," "Sincerely," and "Sincerely yours,".

Signature
If you are typing, skip three or four lines and type your name, placing the first letter of your name under the first letter of the closing.

Neatly sign your name in the space you have left. If you are writing, sign directly under the closing. It is wise to use your proper name, even if you ordinarily never use it. Avoid, for now, using "Shelly" for Rochelle or "Biff" for Vladimir Bifferman. Some applications provide a place for you to write in a nickname you prefer to your actual name. However, until and if that time arrives, let Jimmy or Jamie stay as James and let Peg, Meg, Margie, or Maggie stay as Margaret.

Mailing
The envelope should be addressed with exactly the same words and form as the inside address on the letter. The first line (the director of admissions' name) should be centered both from top to bottom and left to right, with the rest of the address under it.

Photocopy the letter and place the copy in your files. Then, fold the original in *equal* thirds and place it in the envelope. Stamp it, mail it, and wait patiently for a response.

SOME FINAL SUGGESTIONS

DO	*DON'T*
type or write neatly	include sloppy or distracting marks, i.e., erasures, strikeovers, inkblots
use dark-blue or black ink or ribbon	
use 8½"x11" typewriter paper, or stationery (approximately 7"x10")	use small notepaper or loose-leaf paper

DO	DON'T
center the letter on the page	abbreviate if you can spell out the entire word.
leave ample margins, at least 1″ on all sides	
be consistent in style	

FILLING OUT
THE APPLICATION

Recently, many colleges across the country have joined together to issue the same application to all students. This "Common Application" makes your job much easier. You need to prepare only one essay, and with minor variations, submit that same essay to each of the schools that uses the application. Of course, you should submit an original to each, but the preparation time is drastically reduced.

Whether you are filling out the Common Application or a specific application for a particular school, it must not only contain information that presents you as special, it must also look good. Therefore, it's not wise to leave your applications lying around on your desk, or to look them over while you are eating dinner. And don't carry them to school to fill out during study periods. Rumpled or grease-stained pages certainly won't impress an admissions committee. When you finally fill out the forms, complete them as neatly and as carefully as possible. The committee will not appreciate reading anything that has words crossed out or typed over. Among the thousands of applications submitted to admissions committees each year, those that are unappealing in their presentation, no matter how impressive the information they may contain, will undoubtedly be regarded with the same respect as the half-filled coffee containers strewn around their offices as they read through the night.

THE HANDWRITTEN APPLICATION

It would be wise to make two photocopies of the blank application. File one copy and practice filling out the other before you begin on the original. If you have an exceptionally neat handwriting, there is no reason why the application cannot be filled out by hand. Some colleges require it, and it may even make a good impression.

Some hints about making handwritten applications look good:

- Use one pen throughout.
- Don't squeeze. Cut the essay, if necessary, or, if permitted, attach additional pages.
- If the application stock is thin enough, place a heavily ruled pad beneath it and use the rules that appear through the page to keep your essay aligned.
- If the paper is thick, rule very faint lines in pencil and erase them carefully with a soft eraser once your final draft is completed. Be sure the lines are straight. Use a ruler to measure the distance between each line.

THE TYPED APPLICATION

If your handwriting is poor, you can type the application. Typed copy is easier and faster to read. If you can't type, find someone who can do it for you. A poorly typed application is no better than a poorly handwritten one.

As an aside, if you can't type, take a course before you enter college. You will discover that knowing how to type well will save you a great deal of valuable time while you are in college. Better still, learn how to use a word processor, which allows you to edit and rewrite as often as you like without having to retype pages of work. A word processor will make your academic life a lot easier.

THE SHORT ESSAYS

Basically, the first few pages of every application are the same. If you fill out one and file it, it may be used as a model, with minor changes, for all applications. The information generally required includes citizenship, date of birth, education, family background, academic achievements, work experience, and finally, the personal statement. About midway, you will find space in which you are asked to discuss either extracurricular activities, personal activities, or work experiences that have been especially meaningful to you. Because you usually will choose only *one* activity, be sure it is one that will really show who you are. You can refer to your inventory chart (see Chapter 3) to assist you in selecting the one activity that you think best represents you. Like the longer essay, this shorter response creates an image of you as a person. So, choose carefully. Find an original, but not outrageous, way to respond. Be truthful, clear, and informative.

If your application asks you to "Briefly describe any scholastic honors you have won beginning with ninth grade," don't write a list. The college specifically asked you to briefly describe, not briefly list. Therefore, your response might read something like this:

> While in the tenth year, I won second place in an essay contest about neighborhood pride sponsored by the Chamber of Commerce. My essay, entitled "One to One," was about kids helping the elderly by raking leaves in the fall, running errands, shopping in snowy weather. I received a plaque and a $100 bond.

Notice that the paragraph did not just say that the applicant won an award. Instead, it explained the essay so the reader could learn something about how the writer feels about her neighborhood.

>One day this fall, the Music Department chairman announced that before rehearsal began, he was going to conduct elections for president of the school orchestra. Suddenly, my best friend, Josh, shouted out, "I nominate Russ!" Liza followed with, "I second it!" and within minutes, I was unanimously elected. I never felt so wonderful or important before.

Being elected wasn't the main thrust of the paragraph. It was how the writer was touched by his friends' affection for him. Without showing any ego, the writer was clever enough to subtly inform the reader of his tenure in the orchestra, his election as president, and his popularity.

If, under the category of work experience, you are asked to briefly discuss a job you held, you might say something like:

>I thought it was beneath me to be a waiter at a summer resort. But I wanted the money. Sure enough, I made the money. But I also made good friends (it's amazing how sore feet and little sleep bring people together), and I met Dr. Harris, who explained how much I would enjoy studying at Greenbriar College. Well, here I am and if accepted, I plan to take Dr. Harris's class first.

Here the paragraph was not so much about the job but about what the job did for the writer.

You might lift something directly out of your autobiography (see Chapter 3), such as a school extracurricular activity or something of special interest to you, like the entry below:

In my position as Senior Sing leader, I've learned to motivate my cast into frenzies. I may have made a fool of myself, but it was worth it. If I didn't, no one else would either, and Sing would be deadly.

In the paragraph above, we learn about the author's enthusiasm, her ability as a leader, her relaxed attitude, and her concern that Sing be effective.

If asked to discuss your involvement in a nonacademic activity, you might say something like:

Working as the vice-president of the student caucus, I learned to be both a follower and a leader. I learned to take suggestions and to give advice. I learned that sometimes it was better to work alone and other times to be part of a group. These were valuable lessons taught to me by the kids in the caucus, some of whom knew better than I how to work for the common good.

The writer was able to show that he not only successfully served in student government but that he attributes some of his success to his fellow classmates. This shows what a good leader he is.

Do not be afraid to tell the college that you have not chosen a major or do not know what field of study you plan to pursue. You are not alone. Most seventeen-year-olds have not cemented their future ambitions, and the colleges understand.

But, if you have some idea of what course of study you would like to pursue, by all means tell the school what your plans are. Keep in mind that acceptances are never determined by professional objectives. You have the right to change your mind as often as necessary. Below is a sample of what a short essay about career goals might be like:

> Although I do not have a specific professional objective at this time, I am interested in the Human Development and Family Studies program because I am strongly considering a career in either social work or psychology. In order to explore these interests, I spent time visiting a hospital department of psychiatry where I met with the head of the family studies unit, spoke with a bilingual social worker, observed demonstrations of family work, and sat in on a case conference. I also toured an inpatient ward and spoke with several psychologists with different theoretical backgrounds.

Before filling in the short essay, write a scrap copy, revise it, edit it, and have it checked by a parent or other qualified person. Then, on a photocopy of the application, type or neatly write your response in the space provided. If it fits well, it can be transferred to the actual application. If it runs long, edit it again, then type it in on the actual application.

A FEW RECOMMENDATIONS

DO	*DON'T*
practice on a scrap copy.	write directly on the application.
tell the truth.	
be accurate. Check spelling, grammar, dates, places, etc.	include anything that may be misconstrued as something negative about you.
be consistent. If you abbreviate, then do so to all words that require abbreviation.	leave out information. Blank spaces may suggest you do not wish to include something questionable.
type or have someone type for you.	

THE ADDENDUM LETTER

If, after you've sent off your applications, there is need to add information to them (i.e., an award you've won, an office to which you've been elected), feel free to write to the colleges and let them know. Your letter should read something like this:

```
Mr. John Bunnell
Director of Freshman Admissions
Office of Undergraduate Admissions
Old Union, Stanford University
Stanford, CA 94305

Dear Mr. Bunnell:

    Since sending you my application for
admittance to Stanford, I have become art
editor of Kennedy's yearbook and have won
the Auburn Chamber of Commerce "Say No to
```

Drugs" essay contest. Please add those
two items to my application.

Thank you.

If you have an additional photocopy of the application,
you may fill in your new information on the copy. Instead
of asking for the information to be included in your file,
that portion of your letter may read something like this: "I
have listed both honors on a copy of the application. Please
add it to my file."

THE THANK-YOU NOTE

After you have been interviewed by a college, courtesy
dictates that you send the admissions committee a note
of acknowledgment. Though not necessarily the one you
would send, one possible note might be:

Mr. John Bunnell
Director of Freshman Admissions
Office of Undergraduate Admissions
Old Union, Stanford University
Stanford, CA 94305

Dear Mr. Bunnell:

I enjoyed speaking with you on Friday, February 12. Thank you for being
interested in me. I was particularly
grateful that the interview was informal and "low-keyed," because I
usually have to try hard not to spill
coffee during formal occasions.

I think I will enjoy being a student
at Stanford University.

A personal item (in this case, spilling coffee) adds to your being remembered by the admissions personnel. Try, in your letter, to include some personal remark. A sense of humor helps, too.

In general, all your correspondence should be short and to the point. Each letter should be courteous and friendly and reflect a positive personality. Avoid writing "cut and dried," bland letters. Your correspondence represents you as an individual and, if properly written, will help make a good impression.

THE DECLINATION LETTER

It behooves you to send a letter to all schools which have notified you of acceptance but which you have decided not to attend. Good manners and integrity dictate that you relinquish your spot so that a student on the waiting list may replace you.

Mr. John Bunnell
Director of Freshman Admissions
Office of Undergraduate Admissions
Old Union, Stanford University
Stanford, CA 94305

Dear Mr. Bunnell:

Thank you for admitting me to Stanford University. However, I regret that I will be unable to attend. I have decided after careful thought to attend _____ because _____ .

Again, I appreciate your having accepted me.

THE IMPORTANCE OF THE ESSAY

When you fill out the short-answer portion of the application, you are giving the college specific information about your family background, your education, your extracurricular activities, your work experience. Though this information tells the college a lot about you, thousands of students across the country may have similar credentials.

Aside from the interview, which some schools do not even require, the only way the college can get to know you individually is through the essay. Therefore, the essay is a personal communication between you and the school and, as such, must be considered the most important part of the application process. Richard Steele, Duke University's director of admissions, believes it shows an applicant's "maturity, ability to write, and personal qualities which may not be immediately evident from a high school transcript."

The right essay can elevate a good student to a position of special consideration. It can impress the admissions committee that there is something special about the student beyond good grades and numerous activities. Richard W. Haines, director of admissions at Lafayette College, feels that "in many cases the essay is critical. It is really the only part of the application that provides an opportunity for the student to speak for himself in a relatively free-form manner. It is often the feature of the application that we focus on when making distinctions among otherwise similar candidates."

But, oddly enough, this vital part of the application process is postponed more than any other. Perhaps it's because so much of the application is merely filling in the blanks and takes little effort compared to the essay, which takes real concentration. Nevertheless, you should approach the essay early on, because of its importance in the admissions process. Left for last, it becomes a burden that will be dashed off quickly and will probably be read as such. Michael C. Behnke, director of admissions at the Massachusetts Institute of Technology, warns that "someone who submits a sloppy essay is at a severe disadvantage."

Colleges expect that each essay will be well written, with correct grammar, spelling, punctuation, and syntax. Though there is usually no strict length requirement, they expect a fully conceived essay, one that is neither an encyclopedia nor merely a photo caption. What they hope to find, says Richard Steele of Duke, is an essay that shows "a student's ability to organize his or her thoughts, to think clearly." Duke also looks for "intangibles, such as insight, level of maturity, and intellectual depth."

A mere rehashing of the list of school activities taken from the beginning of your application says little. You have already noted what clubs you belong to, what subjects appeal to you, what jobs you've held. But an essay about how one of these clubs, subjects, or jobs has affected you or helped you would be more interesting if it showed something favorable or unusual about you. Nancy Hargrave Meislahn, director of undergraduate admissions, says the admissions committee at Cornell University looks for "active, interesting, motivated, and contributing individuals" in its applicants. What she means is that it's far more interesting to discuss how playing in chess tournaments has influenced your life, or how much you learned about your opponent through playing chess, than to just write, "I was a member of the Chess Team."

If you've earned good grades, if you've received honors, if you've been elected to an office, or if you've been chosen a team captain, feel free to discuss these matters in your essay. Don't be overly modest. The reaction to an essay that whispers will undoubtedly be "C'mon, speak up!" On the other hand, shouting so loudly that it hurts the ears can result in "Aw, shut up!" So, use good judgment. Write proudly yet prudently about your achievements and what they have done for you as a person. But don't forget, the school wants to know more about the person who has achieved some distinction than the achievement itself. The "I did this" and "I did that" essay is usually flat and is sometimes downright objectionable. How you say something is as important as, if not more important than, what you say.

THE IMPORTANCE OF ORIGINALITY

Since you know that hundreds of students are applying for the same seat you are, you need to show that you are as important to the college as the college is to you. The trick is to avoid the commonplace. Think of the tired admissions officers who wade through thousands of essays. They certainly won't look kindly at an essay that's pompous or tedious, which might suggest that the author is that way, too. In short, make your essay light and easy to read. On the other hand, unless you are a natural comic, don't attempt to write a "funny" essay. Forced humor can be less effective than no humor at all. Your goal is to try to impress those tired and beleaguered readers so much that they would like to meet the author.

It should be noted that colleges do not have preconceived ideas about what an essay should say. There is no right or wrong essay, so don't try to anticipate what admissions committees want to read. However, they are unanimous in their plea for an original essay that shows them your individuality. So, be unique. Go out on a limb. Find a new point of view, a fresh approach. However, don't go overboard so that your essay is so esoteric that you paint a picture of yourself as "weird." Feel free to offer your ideas, to discuss your likes and dislikes, and to defend your own opinions. You have earned that right, and the colleges are eager to read about it, as long as you don't sound maudlin, arrogant, or pedantic.

THE CHOICE OF TOPICS

Don't tell everything about yourself. Select one important aspect and confine your discussion to that aspect. If the application offers a choice of essays, select the one about which you can write honestly and creditably. Ms. Meislahn of Cornell asserts that "in many cases it is as much the choice of topic as it is the way the topic is addressed that becomes critical for the selection committee."

Don't try to convince the admissions committee that you are something you aren't. Your essay is not the first that these people have read. If it is fallacious, they will certainly see through it. Just write about yourself and what you know best. Most seventeen-year-olds are not adept at writing intelligently about controversial topics, such as apartheid, the national debt, or arms control. Unless you are one of a very few, avoid undertaking such topics. According to Ms. Meislahn, Cornell, and undoubtedly all other schools, "seeks a student who has sought educational opportunities, created experiences for growth, both academically and extracurricularly, and one who can articulate what he or she has learned from these experiences." Concentrate on her suggestion and avoid topics that may back you into a corner.

If the instructions on the application require that your essay be a specific length, do not exceed that requirement. But, if the application advises you to use an additional page in order to tell more about yourself, it is best not to accept the advice as optional. Regard it as an important opportunity to offer additional ideas or to elaborate on ones you have previously discussed. This option may give you the space and freedom to tell the college anything that, because of the limited space on the application, may have been omitted. This is the place where that one sterling idea may come blazing forth to convince the school that you will be an asset to its freshman class.

THE APPLICATION READERS

It is the responsibility of the committee to form a freshman class out of the very best applicants. Obviously, the more who apply, the more difficult admission is. However, admissions committees do not compare one student's essay to another's. Each applicant is individually considered.

Applications are reviewed in a variety of ways, depending on the institution. For example, at Lafayette College, essays are read by full-time members of the professional admissions staff, who deal with every aspect of the admissions process on a year-round basis. However, at Duke University, essays are read first by two part-time associates who have educational backgrounds and then by an admissions officer.

At Cal Tech, essays are read by an admissions committee consisting of nineteen faculty and staff members. At Amherst College, essays are read by members of the admissions staff, and some are also read by faculty members. And at Williams College, essays are read by three staff members.

Available time and the number of applications to be read must, of necessity, also be an influence on the committee, but the consideration shown to each candidate is never affected by these factors.

THE WEIGHT OF THE ESSAY

In general, applicants are divided into three groups: those who, because of their superior academic strengths (grades and scores), special abilities, and distinctive qualities, are considered immediately acceptable; those who, because of weak grades, lesser abilities, or fewer distinctive qualities, are considered unacceptable; and the largest, middle group, comprising those whose grades, scores, etc., are average or good but not excellent. It is this middle group that occupies most of the admissions personnel's time; it is here that the essay carries its greatest weight.

At Duke, Admissions Director Steele feels that "an extremely poor essay could cause an otherwise excellent applicant to be denied." Director of Admissions Haines of Lafayette College claims that "a strong personal statement can often elevate an applicant from the rejection or alternate list to an acceptable level."

Phillip F. Smith, Williams College's director of admissions, believes "an unfavorable essay or an essay that is dull, sloppy, or bland" written by a superior student "simply represents a missed opportunity."

Finally, Admissions Director Stirling L. Huntley of Cal Tech states, "I don't think that a favorable essay can overcome poor grades, but among those students with the fine grades, a good essay might tip the balance in the case of a student at the margin. A poor essay could certainly have a negative effect on a student's application. By poor, I mean one that indicates indifference, lack of organization, or immaturity on the student's part."

These statements are representative of almost all the colleges and universities across the country. They clearly delineate what they expect and the kind of student they will accept. The right essay can help to convince them you are the applicant they want and need.

WRITER'S BLOCK

What happens if you just can't get into doing the work? Countless writers slip a paper into the typewriter or pull out the yellow pad and then just stare at the blank page. So, if you're facing writer's block, don't panic. All is not lost. Here are some hints that may help you overcome the problem:

- Work where there are no distractions. Find a place away from your kid brother or sister, even away from your parents, and especially away from the telephone. Concentration is important.

- If music helps to relax you, put on the radio or play a tape.
- Start writing the section with which you feel most comfortable. There's no law that says you must start with the opening paragraph and continue in sequence. If you write one decent paragraph, it may spark you to write the next or the one above it. Eventually, you'll put the sections together.
- Set deadlines for yourself. Try to allot time as you would for homework assignments. Create an imaginary deadline and try to meet it.
- Talk out loud or speak into a tape recorder. Sometimes hearing your own voice will give you the impetus to set some lines down on paper.
- Revise something you've already written. Sometimes just sitting down and writing will stimulate you to get on with the important writing.
- Consider that it's only a first draft. Tell yourself it doesn't matter how good it is. You just need to get something down. And that's the truth!

SAMPLE ESSAY QUESTIONS

The following essay topics have appeared on admissions applications during the past few years. Notice how similar they are and how easily they allow you to take control and express yourself freely.

(a) Evaluate a significant experience or achievement that has special meaning for you.
(b) Discuss some issue of personal, local, or national concern and its importance to you.
(c) Indicate a person who has had a significant influence on you, and describe that influence.

Common Application

On the following page, or on an attached sheet, please write a brief essay of 200–500 words. You may choose any topic about which you would like to write: your family, friends, or another person who has had an impact on you; unusual circumstances in your life; the best or worst features of your secondary school; a recent development in your community; a scientific or other problem which you would like to solve; travel or living experiences in other countries; a question we should have asked in our application. Any subject of direct personal importance to you is a good choice.

Harvard-Radcliffe

In a well-written essay of 200–250 words, please tell us of your interest in science or engineering, your educational goals, how Caltech fits into them, and how you see your career developing over the next ten years.

California Institute of Technology

In 200 words or less, describe one of the following:

1. A memorable event you took part in or saw happen. Begin with these words: "I'll never forget . . ."
2. An idea that excited you as soon as you fully understood it. Begin with these words: "When I discovered the meaning of . . ."
3. A conclusion you have reached about a question that has no provable answer. Begin with these words: "After much thought, I have concluded . . ."
4. Something to which you have lost your heart (or maybe your head). Begin with these words: "I'm forced to admit that I'm just crazy about . . ."

Cornell University

In your own handwriting, . . . please write about one or more of the following:

1. Your personal reasons for wanting to attend college and how you think Monmouth College may affect your future.
2. Significant experiences or activities that have affected your current college planning and your readiness to pursue college-level academic study.
3. Other information about yourself you'd like to bring to our attention.

Monmouth College

You have just won a prize for your invention. Describe the invention and why you created it.

Vassar College

Comment on an experience that helped you to discern or define a value that you hold.

Williams College

You are encouraged to write about things that are important to you and tell about yourself. Topics might include your community service, awards you have received, class and student body offices you might have held, school activities (athletics, drama, journalism, musical performances, etc.), work experience, educational interests and goals, personal and career expectations, or anything else of interest to you.

University of California

Give a biographical sketch of at least 200 but not more than 300 words. It is suggested that you include your reasons for wishing to attend the academy, a discussion of your curriculum preference, the development of your interest as a result of your high school classes, hobbies, activities, etc.

The U.S. Merchant Marine Academy

Please let us know something about you that we may not learn from the rest of your application. In the past candidates have used this space in a great variety of ways. They have written about family situations, school or community events to which they have strong reactions, people who have influenced them, significant experiences, intellectual interests, personal aspirations, or— more generally—topics that spring from the life of the imagination. There is no "correct" way to respond to this essay request. In writing about something that matters to you, you will convey to us a sense of yourself.

Yale University

Please answer the following as completely as possible. The personal statements are considered crucial in assessing your verbal communications skills and are highly valued as insights into your individual nature. Your answers to the questions should reflect careful thought.

1. Which single experience do you feel has had the most significant effect on your personal growth? How?

2. Which of your talents and interests would you like to develop further during your college years? Explain fully.

Guilford College

Select your favorite quotation, or one that holds special importance for you, and comment upon its significance.

Stanford University

GETTING ORGANIZED

2

TAKING INVENTORY OF YOURSELF

It's not likely that you will be able to construct a well-focused essay without some organization of the facts and opinions to be included. We recommend and will show you the following method of organization:

1. The construction of a basic autobiographical outline.
2. The development of that outline into a fully annotated inventory chart.
3. The development of an autobiography based upon the inventory chart.

The purpose of the above method is to give you an organization for the most in-depth look at yourself, because what you want to reflect is what the admissions committee should see. And it's important for them to see the best part of you in the sharpest focus possible.

THE AUTOBIOGRAPHICAL OUTLINE

On a sheet of paper, respond to the following topics. Spelling, grammar, etc., don't count this time.

Biology Department, Earlham College, Indiana

1. *Basic facts about your family*
Occupations; number of people; how you fit into that group. Details can be included if they're interesting. For instance, special relationships with family members, responsibilities at home, how family members or exceptional or unusual circumstances may have influenced your interests, goals, and needs.

2. *Basic facts about school*
Subject areas you enjoy most, areas in which you excel, areas in which you may have problems. Does your academic program reflect your future goals? How or why not? Have you pursued studies outside of school based on a subject you studied in school? Was there a teacher who particularly impressed you? In what extracurricular activities were you involved? What *specifically* did you do? How have they benefited the school or community? Are they related in any way to your interests or goals? In what way?

3. *Basic facts about specific interests or goals*
What occupies your spare time (music, athletics, hobbies, etc.)? What specifically have you done in pursuit of those interests? How are they related to your personal goals and/or future plans? What do you expect to prepare for? (If you have not decided, say so.) Are there choices you've considered? Why do you think you'd like such work?

4. *Basic facts about your work experience*
What jobs did you have? What specifically did you do? Specify whether they were paying, nonpaying, after school, summer employment. What did you learn in skills, self-awareness, understanding of the needs of others? How was this work related to future goals/plans?

5. *Optional—other valuable basic facts*
What person and/or experience has had the greatest in-

fluence on you? In what way? What has been your most significant achievement? What goals and ideals are important in your life? Why are you applying to this particular college (reputation, special department, recommendation of friends or relatives)?

If you take this exercise seriously, you will have a compendium of facts about yourself that will form the basis of what will ultimately reveal who you are to the admissions committee.

OTHER POINTS
OF VIEW

Now take this exercise one step further. You can get a more three-dimensional picture of yourself by examining perspectives other than your own. Have three people write about you based on the same outline. Where some facts do not apply, ask if they would substitute an experience they might have shared with you that either clarified your personality or gave them insight into a side of you and/ or your goals they knew nothing about. Sure, it will take some time, but if they're the right people they won't mind. They can be friends, a parent, a relative, or a teacher. This document is informal. Your only objective here is to gather information you may not be aware of, to make your image more vivid.

Honesty, specific information, and a positive attitude are what matter here, so ask these three people to follow the same guidelines you followed.

Again, once collected, the information becomes a part of your basic autobiographical outline. You can eliminate those parts that you think aren't important. But be aware that you may be seeing things about yourself for the first time. Therefore, be fair. What may strike you as negative may be useful after all, if you can turn it around to a positive learning experience.

THE INVENTORY CHART

Once you've collected the information, it's time to make an inventory chart. The chart will become a "data base" from which you may draw when writing your autobiography and will eventually be used as a source for any of the possible essay topics. Although you certainly may design your own, the following is a possible format.

Now, here is how you fill in the boxes.

INVENTORY CHART

SUBJECT	FACTS	OBSERVATIONS

Under *Subject*, enter the first subject area to be covered. For instance, in Topic 1, the subject is *Family*. In Topic 2, the subject is *School*.

Under *Facts*, enter *just* the facts that fall within the subject category. You should have four sets of facts; yours, and the facts gathered from the three other people. For instance, in Topic 1, *Family*, the facts entered are how many people are in your family, what responsibilities you have at home, and those family members who have influenced you.

Under *Observations*, enter your viewpoints and those of the others about each of the facts listed. For instance, in Topic 1, *Family*, the facts are that there are five family members (father, mother, and two sisters). The observations are that the father is easygoing, the mother is meticulous, and both sisters are role models. This area of the chart will help you to distinguish the facts from how you feel about them.

A completed inventory chart is provided so that you can understand what goes where on your own inventory chart. Read through it before you start filling in yours.

Your completed inventory chart has now organized the facts and observations about your life in such a way that you can retrieve the information quickly and easily.

THE AUTOBIOGRAPHY

Now, with all your basic ammunition assembled, you are ready to construct your autobiography. The following sample was created based upon the inventory chart you just read. It is meant to help you see how the chart is used.

I don't recall our family ever being in need of anything, although my mom did remind us often that Dad worked two jobs. My sisters and I shared housecleaning, shopping, and laundry responsibilities according to a

FAMILY
LIFE

FACTS	OBSERVATIONS
Five Family Members:	
Mother—real estate agent Father—master plumber Two sisters—one twin, one two years older	Mother—good cook, meticulous. Father—easygoing, more tolerant. Both sisters are role models. Both sisters are prettier than I am. I'm more introspective, but I like to have fun as much as the next per- son. Little competitiveness with twin. Dad always takes us everywhere and reads encyclopedias for fun. Mother taught us to love reading.
Responsibilities:	
Shared cleaning duties, entire house, my room Shopping or laundry Bringing home good marks	Mother wanted us to learn household skills—a little outmoded.
Family Influences to Help Achieve Goals:	
Father—You can do whatever you want. Mother—Always do your best.	Made me a leader in school. Made hard tasks easier to tackle.

INVENTORY CHART

SCHOOL LIFE	FACTS	OBSERVATIONS
	Subjects in Which I Excel:	
	English Foreign language Biology Theatre Athletics	I want to be an actress, teach acting, be a doctor, philosopher, or director. All those subjects will be helpful in achieving goals, but also like to study unusual creatures. Very competitive.
	Subjects in Which I Have Trouble:	
	Geometry	Almost a block here. Good in algebra involving intricate thinking, but more like a language. Can't understand applications in geometry.
	Related Study Outside of School	Metropolitan Opera Ballet School. Read a great deal—more than any of my friends. Love to read about sharks.
	Extracurricular Activities:	
	Cheerleader captain Sing leader Sophomore-class president	Make loads of friends. Learn to listen and get along with others. Learn to motivate. Learn to lead—benevolent dictator.

INVENTORY CHART

WORK EXPERIENCE	FACTS	OBSERVATIONS
	After School and Weekends:	
	Work at uncle's clothing store	Like the extra money but spend it on gifts for others.
		Meet interesting people.
		Have learned about inventory and meeting sales goals. Learned about stress if goals weren't met and how to write sales reports.
		Sometimes I sell and help people to feel better about themselves.
		Also makes me feel good that people trust and believe in me enough to pay money for goods I help them with.
	Summer Camp:	
	Counselor	Like to work with kids.
	Theatre counselor	Help them to achieve goals.
		Love working in theatre, building sets, performing, and acting.

45■

INVENTORY CHART

SPECIAL INTERESTS/ FUTURE GOALS	FACTS	OBSERVATIONS
	Theatre Art Swimming	Attend theatre but would rather participate as a leader rather than a follower, but am a good team player. Love to paint—wish I were better at it. Love the feel of freedom of interacting with water—feel as if I'm flying.
	Relation to Future Goals: Teacher Leader Doctor	If I become teacher, politician, or doctor, all above skills will be helpful for each. All performed before an audience. Swimming empowers me—if I could relate feelings I have during swimming to everyday tasks, they probably would be easier.
	Why Would I Like Work?	All demonstrate leadership, initiative, some form of creativity, and interaction with people.

INVENTORY CHART

ADDITIONAL INFORMATION	FACTS	OBSERVATIONS
	Experiences or People Who Have Influenced Me:	
	My father	His tolerance, his patience, his quest for knowledge, his fairness, his humor, his dimples when he's angry, his smile when he's pleased. Help me to become a leader, to realize no challenge is impossible. To never give up.
	Winning an Important Election	First didn't want to run, but was challenged by a competitor. Took up the challenge, used my "people skills," theatrical skills, sense of humor and fairness, and won.
	Losing an Important Race	Hard to be team member and when it was up to me to finish race, I failed the team. But team made me feel better.

INVENTORY CHART

ADDITIONAL INFORMATION	FACTS	OBSERVATIONS
	Goals and Ideals Important in Life:	Being dishonest is anathema to me.
	Be successful and happy in whatever I do	It has been instilled in me by my father.
	Be honest	Once I stole a magazine and had to return it, explain my be-
	Try to be fair	havior to shopkeeper, and pay for it out of my own money.
		Still hard for me to be fair.
	Why I Am Applying to College	Looking for excellent liberal arts, especially theatre, and maybe science depart-
	Academics	ment.
	Campus life	Sister's friend attended. Mother's friend's son attended. Heard about it in newspaper be- cause of research depart- ment.

chart I devised. Although it seemed equal in the division of labor, any one of us could barter our chores if the other had money or a dress we all wanted to wear, or if one could do the other sister's homework. I bartered with the best, but I didn't mind the dusting because I knew I wasn't going to choose homemaking as a career. My dad instilled in all of us, and especially in me, that I could do anything I wanted if I tried hard enough. It was his influence plus the support of my mother and sisters that made it easy for me to become a leader in school and earn excellent grades. Mom always encouraged me to be the best I could at everything, and dating was not as important to me as good grades were.

At school I excel in English, Spanish, biology, theatre, and athletics. All will put me in good stead if I actually intend to pursue an acting, teaching, or medical career because it seems to me that each of those careers requires the ability to get up and perform. And I do that naturally. Becoming a good athlete is not a career goal, but it teaches me to be competitive, and in each of my career goals it pays to be competitive. I do have a mental block when it comes to geometry. I could figure out algebra, because it is almost like the language of math, but I can't understand how geometry applies to any of my experiences. You could say it's all Greek to me!

One thing I know I can thank my mom for is my love of reading. I read tons of books— more than any of my friends. Consequently, I learn a great deal. My interest now is in reading about sharks, the most feared creatures in the sea. Since I swim frequently, I thought it would be a good idea to learn about sharks.

At school, I'm cheerleader captain and Senior Sing leader. I was sophomore-class president and Sing leader as well. It just seems natural because I make friends easily. My dad taught me to be tolerant and try to get along with others. In my position as Sing leader, I've learned to motivate my class into frenzies. I may make a fool of myself. But that's okay. If I didn't, no one else would follow.

Although I'm not very fond of the work ethic (getting up early, riding to work, and punching a time clock), I like the extra money. But I often spend more on gifts for others than I do on myself. At work, I did learn about stress on the job. Since my uncle was manager of a large men's clothing store, he had to meet weekly and monthly sales goals. I would notice the change in his posture and attitude when sales fell behind goals. Sometimes, when he was in a particularly foul mood, he'd let me write the sales reports. Although the overall theme may have been negative, I'd always try to end the report on a positive note by saying something like, "Next month we anticipate much better sales performance." In addition, I enjoyed helping customers and especially enjoyed it when my point of view helped to make a sale.

During the summer, I worked as a general counselor, where I headed a group of fourteen-year-olds. I liked being in a position of motivating them and always felt I left a

bit of myself with them. Last year, I became
a swimming counselor. That was most enjoya-
ble because some kids begin the summer
afraid of the water. But by summer's end,
they usually feel the same way I do about
swimming.

When I'm swimming, I feel as if I'm
flying. It empowers me and I hope I can
translate that feeling when I am performing
other tasks, especially in relation to my
future goals. I hope that rush of exhilara-
tion I receive through swimming will affect
me positively. In any case, whatever
professional goals I may pursue, they will
always demonstrate my capabilities in lead-
ership, initiative, creativity, and love of
people.

My choice of Oberlin College was based
upon my career goals and the extensive liberal arts curriculum offered. I think I
would make an excellent addition to the
freshman class. My mother's friend's daughter reported to me that campus life is relaxed, not snobbish, and mostly fun. That's
a good atmosphere in which I can excel because it's similar to the home atmosphere in
which I grew up.

The above autobiography is a warmly written introduction to the home life of the student. She has woven
her family influences into the formulation of her career
goals. As a first attempt, it is quite good. However, it is
much too long, and there are a number of syntax errors,
redundancies, and punctuation faults. But that does not
matter at this point because the autobiography is just a
reference tool. No one but the author sees it.

The next two autobiographies were based on the writers' own inventory charts. Because the lives of these authors are different, the information contained in their inventory charts is also different, even though both authors followed the same format. Additionally, there are certain aspects in both autobiographies that are more important than other aspects. While the first autobiography you read emphasized the influence of family life, these next two emphasize different influences.

Throughout my life I've always been awed by the way the human body functions with respect to its thoughts, emotions, and its homeostatic mechanisms for longevity. It is for this reason that I have related many of my in-school and extracurricular pursuits to studying and participating in activities related to the sciences.

During the summer of 1985 I volunteered at the Forensic Institute of Medicine (N.Y.C. Office of the Chief Medical Examiner). There I tested the blood, urine, and liver of the deceased for different drugs by using various laboratory techniques (i.e., thin layer chromatography and gas chromatography), to determine the cause of death. I also viewed many autopsies of bodies from drowning victims to homicide victims and learned that side of medicine where "Quincy" leaves off.

Two years later I attended the Cornell University Advanced Placement Summer Program. I took two courses: Oral Communications and Psychology, the Cognitive Approach. The first course, dealing with public speaking, can help me relate to people and understand various social situations. This will prove especially benefi-

cial in the medical profession, which I'm
pursuing, where the doctor-patient relationship is of great importance. The latter
course, dealing with attention, memory,
perception, and learning, also proved to be
helpful in these respects, in that it ex-
plores many aspects of the human mind.

Mathematics motivates me academically as
much as science and medicine. It is for this
reason that I have held the position of captain of Midwood's championship Math Team.
My interest in science and mathematics led
me to enter the 1985 and 1986 N.Y.C. Math
Fair held at Pace University. In the former
I presented a paper entitled, "Mathemati-
cal Analysis of the Laws of Gravitation"
and won second place (silver medal) in
N.Y.C.

Besides participating in the Math Fair,
I've been a contributor to <u>Argus</u>, our school
magazine. My short story about a ventrilo-
quist was based on my interest in ventriloquism, a skill I have been developing since
I was about ten, when my uncle gave me a
dummy for a birthday present. On occasion, I
perform at parties and at children's wards
of hospitals. But, I have no intention of
pursuing ventriloquism as a career. It's
just fun.

To relax, I enjoy weight lifting, which I
do on the Nautilus in my basement. My dad and
I work out together a few nights a week. On
Saturday mornings, I also attend karate
class. I'm not particularly interested in
karate as a type of self-defense (though I
don't deny its usefulness). I am more interested in the discipline it helps me develop

and the sense of inner comfort I find it
gives me.

As for the future, I hope to become a doc-
tor and, if all goes well, to specialize in
surgery.

In the above autobiography, the writer talks mostly
about his academic life. Though impressive, it appears to
be a bit too serious and somewhat stuffy. If any of it were
to be used in an essay, it would need to have added to
it a spark of personality, which is only seen at the end.
Selling yourself is one thing; overselling is boring. When
the autobiography is to be used as the basis for the essay,
the salient features of a student's life are not to be ignored.
However, they need to be interspersed with a more personal touch.

<u>Kowloon</u> means "nine dragons" in
Chinese. My mother, father, and the five
children live on Kowloon's Peak, a penin-
sula in Hong Kong which from a distance
seems to have nine dragons stretching
across the mountaintop.

Each morning I come down from the peak to
attend Maryknoll Convent School, an American Catholic high school. Although we are
taught by American nuns, the method of education is based on the British Matricula-
tion Board. When I was younger, I had a difficult time mastering Chinese. Even though
I am Chinese, I found the literature and
grammar very difficult. So instead, I became fluent in French, and even today feel
more comfortable speaking French than
Chinese.

A few years ago my parents took my brother
Alexander and me to visit my eldest sister

who lives with her husband in Paris. It was
an ideal chance to perfect my French. My
other sister, Jean, is a biology major at
Pomona College in California. My other
brother, Michael, works for my father.

And that brings me to the reason I want to
attend the University of Michigan. My father was educated there, as was my brother
Andrew. And my sister at Pomona is planning
to do her graduate work there. From hearing
so much about Michigan from both of them, I
feel I know the school already. My father
organized the first Chinese fraternity at
Michigan. My brother was also a member. They
are both architects. My father, who worked
with Buckminster Fuller for many years,
built the first geodesic dome in Hong Kong,
and my brother created China's first pre-
fabricated housing.

However, I'm not interested in architec-
ture. I plan to major in English literature
and look forward to my first classes. My
only hesitation is that I have never lived
in a place where it snows. I have been to
America before, to study at a girls' school
for the summer, but I was in southern California, where it is always summer. Being
there alone was an adventure, but my parents
have always allowed all their children to do
adventurous things. So I look forward to
coming to America and to Michigan in particular. I hope it will be one more adventure.

This third autobiography, though it follows an inventory chart and has some very interesting things to say,
like the author, meanders all over the globe. It has no
focus. At this point, the autobiography is clearly not usable

as an essay. It has no "hook." The author will need to choose one of the areas she discusses as the focus of her essay. She can write about her mountain, her primary education, her large family, her interest in America, or her enthusiasm for the University of Michigan. The important thing is, she must find something solid on which to formulate an essay.

Similarly, after reviewing your own autobiography, you ought to be able to find a hook, a unique idea that you don't suspect will appear in anyone else's essay. One way to find it is to consider, merely as an exercise, what advertising agencies do to promote a product.

You have just read three selections that were developed from outlines through inventory charts and finally into autobiographies. Along with reading these three, you've formulated your own autobiography. It is hoped yours is focused and contains the kind of vibrant information that can be used to write a winning essay.

MARKETING YOURSELF

Advertisers pay for thirty, fifteen, or ten seconds of radio or TV time to communicate a message about their product. Because advertising time is so expensive, the most important feature of the product must be stressed and the message communicated in such a way that it will make the audience sit up and take notice.

Now, imagine yourself as the product. What can you say about yourself in ten seconds that will make the admissions board take notice of you?

Try the following exercise: Use a timer and see just how long ten seconds is. Using that time frame as your guide, tell something about yourself that makes you special. Have someone actually time your presentation.

The ten-second spot encapsulates something unusual about yourself. It can become a perfect starting place for an essay, or, if written well, it can be an effective opening sentence.

Let's take our exercise a step further. Using your inventory chart, select an ability, skill, or accomplishment that you think will differentiate you from the rest of the applicants and synthesize those attributes into a thirty-second television spot. While a real spot may use bold, graphic, colorful visuals, you are limited to just your writing. You must learn to appeal to the reader's visual sensibilities by finding those words that show, not merely tell.

The following is a completed thirty-second spot extended from an idea originally conceived in the first autobiography you read beginning on page 42. Notice how the writer's enthusiasm about swimming was converted into a vivid statement about how she perceives life.

I sometimes think I should have been a fish. Swimming unleashes my life-force. There is nothing more invigorating than slicing through the water, an alien environment nature has not destined to be ours. I can barrel through, I can dive, I can turn somersaults in the water and the water bolsters me and frees my spirit. I can turn that alien environment into a place I belong.

There is no rush quite like the ebullience, the joy, the power I feel in the water. I wish there were a way of retaining that rush so that anything I want to do outside the water gives me the same kind of high.

Now let's take a look at a young man who's at the top of his class. He wrote the autobiography starting on page 52. We commented that the autobiography needed a spark of personality to become the basis of an essay. We think the writer found that spark, or hook, by developing a thirty-second spot based on his interest in ventriloquism. Though it wasn't an important part of his autobiography, look how he's used it now:

> I have a repeating nightmare of myself as a surgeon. There I am in the operating room, a patient, suffering from some near-fatal disease, lying in front of me. I ask for a scalpel, but no one responds. I ask again. Still no response. Finally, I look up, about to reprimand my inefficient staff, when I notice Charlie McCarthy on my left, Jerry Mahoney on my right, and Lambchop sitting on the patient's big toe. I think my subconscious is telling me something. Somehow my two interests, medicine and ventriloquism, just don't blend.

Both thirty-second spots draw immediate interest. In fact, they both could serve as opening paragraphs of actual essays.

Although this may take a little effort, the benefits of having prepared a good introductory paragraph for your essay are worth the effort. Furthermore, this is one writing skill that will serve you well throughout your college years. For, no matter what type of essay you write, if you can't grab a reader in the first paragraph, you may have lost that reader for good.

GETTING INTO WRITING IT

3

Once you have all your applications, assemble them and copy down all the essay topics, each on a separate index card. Note the name of the college on the card. Be aware that many colleges request similar essay topics. Therefore, it may not be necessary to write an essay for every one of them. One might suffice for a number of schools.

FOCUSING

Let's look at the big picture. You have before you your topic cards, your inventory, and your autobiography. Basically, everything you need is there. Now you begin the process of making the most effective use of this information.

With the topic cards in hand, read your autobiographical and inventory data. Note on each topic card those salient facts about yourself you think provide the best examples to answer each specific essay topic.

For example, if an essay topic card asks you to write about an experience of lasting value and your autobiography contains information about spending a day with your congressman, jot this information down on that essay card. If another card asks about an extracurricular activity that has helped you to grow and your autobiography contains information about your participation in student government, jot that down on the essay card.

Student taking a test

Transfer *only* that information which is germane to the essay topic, nothing more. Irrelevant information clouds the focus of your essay.

Continue the same process for each of the essay cards. If, for instance, you have eight essay topics, you will end up with eight index cards, each containing the main idea of a possible essay.

Some people (but not many) have the knack of being able to sit down and write without any prior thinking. Others need some preparation. We recommend you prepare an informal outline so you will be sure you have a beginning, middle, and end. Your outline need only be a list of the various items to be included in your essay in the order they should appear. It's just to keep you on track.

THE OPENING SENTENCE

Let's begin at the beginning. Opening sentences must capture the reader's attention. If they are dull, the reader will not want to continue. Consider the following suggestions.

Instead of saying "I am special," demonstrate that you are by saying something like: "There just isn't any more room on my shelf to put another trophy."

Instead of saying "I'd like to attend Campus University . . ." why not say, "I have been dreaming of being an artist since I was ten, and now that I'm ready to really study intensively, I know that Campus University will offer the kind of education I need and want."

Instead of saying "My favorite person is . . ." you could begin by offering a glimpse of the person by saying: "I don't remember him ever raising his voice or ever looking askance at any student. What I do remember is him saying, 'I guess I need to help you more. Let's have lunch together tomorrow. Finding the roots of a fourth-degree equation isn't easy. But you'll get it.'"

Instead of beginning an autobiographical sketch with: "I was born in 19__," find a key moment in your life *(en medias res)* and fill in incidentals as you go: "Everyone stood up and cheered when the principal handed me the Centerville Middle School Student of the Year Award. There I was, all fourteen years of me, about to show those big shots at Adams High School how this superkid with a 98.3 average was going to stand them on their ear. However, by the end of my sophomore year, this 'super-kid's' grades were subaverage."

Notice how each of these *shows* instead of *tells*. They are the kind of opening sentences that will stimulate the reader to want to read more about you.

THE OPENING PARAGRAPH

Let's turn an opening sentence into an opening paragraph. One of the best methods is to develop each paragraph around a strong topic sentence (the main idea) and then support that topic sentence with details. Here's an example:

> As editor of my school's yearbook I was faced with these problems: how to get the graduates to promptly submit the quotations that caption their photographs, how to spark the staff to sell ads, and how to convince the faculty advisor to allow the students to exercise more control over the contents.

The first sentence in this paragraph is the topic sentence. It tells us that the author is going to write about how he overcame specific problems inherent in his position as editor. The three problems listed will be discussed more fully in the ensuing paragraphs.

Let's look at another paragraph that begins with a topic sentence:

I have always been warned that
physical conditioning alone is insuf-
ficient preparation for a professional athlete. With this in mind, I
have been careful to monitor my diet,
to avoid the use of any type of drug or
stimulant, and to remain calm in
stressful situations.

From this paragraph we learn that the author is about to delineate the three rules he has followed to improve his athletic skill. Each of his next three paragraphs should discuss one of the precautions he takes. The first should discuss his diet, the second his avoidance of drugs, and the third his sound mind.

The topic sentence needn't always be first to be effective. In the following paragraph, it was held for last:

The first stop was London. I was
fascinated to be in the capital of the
country responsible for the roots of
my language. The second stop was Madrid.
It was warm, exotic, different from
what I had expected. And the last stop
was Paris. It was here that I learned a
lesson in international diplomacy I
will never forget.

Because the topic sentence is last, we the readers will be escorted right into the second paragraph. We know we are about to learn the writer's lesson. And because the first paragraph is so interesting, we are eager to read on.

These opening paragraphs contain strong topic sentences supported by details that outline what the body of the essay will contain. By using the topic-sentence approach, you will always have a ready-made structure that will help you to develop your entire essay and lead you to a logical conclusion.

INTRODUCTORY PARAGRAPHS

The topic-sentence approach is a good one, but not the only one. Your opening sentences need not necessarily give away your entire essay. What they must do is "grab" the reader and convince him or her to read further. Such sentences or paragraphs are known as "introductory."

As an example, the opening of the "My Favorite Person" essay (on page 61) never even mentions the subject's name, though there are hints that the essay is about to exalt the virtues of the writer's math teacher. The subliminal thesis is there; the topic sentence is not.

Now let's see how we move from the opening paragraph to the body of the essay.

DEVELOPMENT PARAGRAPHS

If you've written an effective opening paragraph, you can be assured that the reader will be enticed into reading the remainder of the essay. One way to insure this is to find a key word or group of words in the first paragraph and carry it or them into the second.

If, as in one of our samples, your first paragraph ends with, "However, by the end of my sophomore year, this 'superkid's' grades were subaverage," you might begin with, "Subaverage, my eye! I was flunking everything and I didn't know why." The word "subaverage" was carried into the second paragraph as a transition. Or the author could have written something like, "I studied every night, did all my homework, but, no matter what, I couldn't get a passing grade." Here the word "grade" was carried through as a transition and also served to further develop the tone of the essay.

Let's go back and see how the authors of our sample opening paragraphs developed their ideas. The young man who wrote about his trip to Europe goes on to say:

> While walking along the streets of Paris, I came upon a beautiful, lush, green park surrounded by a gate. A sign on the gate said "Jardins de Luxembourg"—Luxembourg Gardens. I was certainly impressed by the gardens, but, more important, I was hopelessly lost. However, under the sign was a police officer. I walked over and asked her the way to the Boulevard St.-Germain, a street with which I was familiar. As I began to speak, she interrupted with a pleasant "Bonjour." I was somewhat taken aback. When was the last time an American police officer said hello to you? I nodded and continued, but she again interjected, this time a little more forcefully, "Bonjour." I continued my request. But again she cut in with "Bonjour." Her smile was beginning to fade.
>
> It suddenly hit me; she was teaching me a lesson in courtesy. I responded with "Bonjour," and the police officer was more than happy to show me the way, speaking slowly and distinctly so I would understand every French word.

The author has effectively developed his theme about learning a lesson in diplomacy—his original intent in the opening paragraph. His technique was to introduce his topic and then to demonstrate his theme by using a narrative.

The author with professional sports aspirations continues with:

For me, eating is not just a way to calm hunger pangs. It is a time to re-fuel. Whether it is breakfast, lunch, or dinner, I select foods that help me to get through the day and sleep well at night. They are always high in fiber and carbohydrates and low in fats. When I want something sweet, I opt for a fruit or a fruit-flavored yogurt.

As the commercial says, "Life is stimulating enough." While that may not be true in all circumstances (including my English literature class), I avoid the use of artificial stimulants like caffeine in coffee or pop. Instead, I drink plenty of fruit juices. When I have the time and if I want to treat myself real well, I'll concoct something in our blender. The bananas, papaya, sesame seeds, and natural honey leave behind quite a mess. Mom calls me the Sloppy Health Gourmet. But she always says, "Leave some for me." Unfortunately, she'll have the fruit drink in one hand and a cigarette in the other. I wish there was a way I could make her understand how much damage she does to herself.

If I'm under a great deal of stress because of an upcoming test or an important competition, I have two ways

```
to relieve the tension. The first is
exercise--jogging always works! An-
other stress reliever for me is music.
Hurray for my Walkman!
```

Again, the author has followed the structure of his opening paragraph. He has cited examples of what he eats to keep in good physical condition. He relates his experience with natural stimulants and follows with some interesting examples of how he reduces stress. Citing specific examples is an excellent way of developing ideas that are introduced in the opening paragraph.

CONCLUSIONS

Once you've developed your ideas in the body of the essay, so that the reader has a clear picture of who you are and what you are thinking, you're ready to present your concluding paragraph. This paragraph should rein-force your initial thesis, leaving the reader with a lasting impression. Caution: never conclude with lines like: "That's why Mr. Jones is my favorite teacher," or "That's why I want to go to Campus University." Sentences like these are obvious signals that you did not know how to resolve your ideas or that you were not prepared to draw a logical conclusion.

The best way to show you how to sum up an essay is to examine the conclusions of the two samples that we just developed. The student who wrote about Paris con-cludes:

```
    How ironic that it was in France,
where they speak a language I under-
stand fairly well but one with which I
do not readily identify, that I
learned my lesson: courtesy is cour-
tesy in any language.
```

See how this young man logically develops his conclusion as a natural outgrowth of the preceding narrative and, at the same time, reinforces his opening statement by relating it to the fact that French is not his native language?

And now for the athlete. He concludes by saying:

> Because of my diet, my avoidance of stimulants, and my actions to eliminate stress in its earliest stages, I am free to train my body to perform the necessary skills which will ultimately enable me to reach my goal of becoming a professional baseball player. I jog 5 miles every morning before school. After class, I practice with the team, and, when I don't have a great deal of homework, I spend an additional hour with my coach, developing my pitching arm. Every Saturday morning I'm at the field warming up, waiting for the rest of the team to arrive, and then we play ball. My coach thinks that, with enough training, I'll make the pros. On a good day, when I've pitched a winning game, I like to believe he's right.

For his conclusion, the author returns to his original thesis about being a pro athlete. This method is almost foolproof because it systematically creates a well-constructed essay that logically develops from beginning to end.

The process we've just discussed is technically correct. But another technique that can be employed is one in which the thirty-second spot is used.

USING THE COMMERCIAL

Let's reexamine one of the thirty-second spots that was developed in Chapter 2.

> I sometimes think I should have been a fish. Swimming unleashes my life-force. There is nothing more invigorating than slicing through the water, an alien environment nature has not destined to be ours. I can barrel through, I can dive, I can turn somersaults in the water and the water bolsters me and frees my spirit. I can turn that alien environment into a place I belong.
>
> There is no rush quite like the ebullience, the joy, the power I feel in the water. I wish there were a way of retaining that rush so that anything I want to do outside the water gives me the same kind of high.

That last sentence is a perfect transition into the body of the essay. Here's the next paragraph:

> I want to explore areas in which I have interests but no familiarity. Mathematics has been my bête noire. I want to apply the same enthusiasm I have for swimming to calculus and finite math. There must be a way for me to knock down the cement dam that prevents me from understanding the flow of this quantifiable language of the universe. I'll find it. I know I will. And when I do, I expect the same rush,

the same freedom I find when I am swimming.

By following through with the "rush" concept that ends
her second paragraph, the author successfully finishes
her essay by discussing how the college of her choice
will benefit her. Notice how she continues the use of the
overall "swimming/water" metaphor to bring her to a logical, impressive conclusion.

In order to help me in my search for
the elusive "rushes of life," I realize I'll need to have a very strong
liberal arts foundation. Since I have
not fully determined what it is I ultimately will be, the opportunity to
be exposed to an ocean of information
becomes primary to me. Perhaps that is
why I selected Oberlin as the institution I would like to attend. Oberlin's
wide selection of curriculum offer-
ings allows me that freedom to tread
in unknown waters. I don't know if
I'll be swimming upstream or if I'll
feel comfortable swimming with the
current. I just know that Oberlin
gives me the feeling that it's a place
where it's safe for me to test the
water.

Now let's go back to the surgeon-ventriloquist. Here's
his thirty-second spot:

I have a repeating nightmare of myself as a surgeon. There I am in the
operating room, a patient, suffering
from some near-fatal disease, lying
in

front of me. I ask for a scalpel, but
no one responds. I ask again. Still no
response. Finally, I look up, about to
reprimand my inefficient staff when I
notice Charlie McCarthy on my left,
Jerry Mahoney on my right, and
Lambchop sitting on the patient's big
toe. I think my subconscious is telling me something. Somehow my two interests, medicine and ventriloquism,
just don't blend.

He ends his first paragraph by saying that his two
interests are contradictory. But if we look back at his autobiography, we see he clearly states, "I have no intention
of pursuing ventriloquism as a career." Therefore, it is
logical that he continues by saying:

Voice throwing has no place in a
surgical pavillion. Can you imagine
my walking into a room to tell a patient that I have successfully removed a duodenal obstruction and she
hears my voice come out of her bedpan?
How's that for bedside manner? It just
won't work. So I guess I'll have to
leave ventriloquism here in New York
and concentrate on being a premed student at Harvard.

He ends with the following paragraph:

While surgical ventriloquism is a
nightmare to me, enrolling at Harvard
would be a dream come true. I'd be the
first in my family to enter an Ivy Lea-
gue school and that, of course, would

please my parents. But what would please me more is that I would have the opportunity to obtain the best training I can in my preparation for a medical career. Moreover, the kind of atmosphere at Harvard is probably conducive to attempting the unorthodox. It's not totally unrealistic to assume then that Harvard may show me my bedside manner might include using a Jerry Mahoney dummy to make the patient feel more comfortable.

Here again, the author develops his concluding paragraph by moving from enrolling at Harvard to what he anticipates he will gain from attending the institution. He ends by returning to his opening remarks and uses his enthusiasm for ventriloquism as a conclusion.

Now, pick up one of your index cards, read the essay topic, skim the notes you have written beneath it, jot down a scrap outline of the topics to be included, and start writing. You should not find this too difficult because you're in control of your ideas and can concentrate on the writing itself.

GETTING
A GRIP

4

PERFECTING YOUR
WRITING TECHNIQUE

Good writing is not only imaginative, it is also crisp, clean, and to the point. From the hundreds of thousands of words available, you the writer need to choose just the right ones so that your essay effectively says all that you want it to say.

The key to good writing is good editing, which means revising and rewriting if necessary. You want to be sure that your reader is aware of what points you are making. Admissions personnel are not about to say, "I think he means this," or "I guess her point is that." Unlike your teacher, they do not correct essays and ask for rewrites. Therefore, you need to say it correctly the first time. What the committee will not know is that the paper they see for the "first time" may well be one that you've revised for the fifth time. And there's nothing wrong with that. The more critical you are of yourself, the less critical anyone else will be.

Before you ask your teacher or another knowledge-able person to comment on your essay, rewrite it so that it's the best possible essay you think it can be. Even professional authors pass along their work to friends for criticism before they submit the manuscript to their editors. And even then, their editors ask for rewrites.

Chambers Building, Davidson College, North Carolina

Be prepared for criticism and accept it graciously. The person who says "This is fine. Type it up and mail it out" probably didn't read your essay carefully.

Let's take a look at some common weaknesses and how they can be corrected.

ACTIVE/PASSIVE VOICE

To make your essays sound more authoritative, use the active voice because it emphasizes the action performed by the subject. In general, your essay will be about you. If you are the subject, you become stronger in the active voice. For instance:

Active: Pharmacists do not mix compounds.
Passive: Compounds are not mixed by pharmacists.

In the active voice, pharmacists instigate the action. In the passive voice, compounds become the subject. *Do not mix* is a far stronger verb than *are not mixed by*.

Use the passive voice only when necessary, such as when the one responsible for the action is unknown or unimportant. For example: "The class was canceled before we arrived." It doesn't matter who canceled the class.

WORDINESS

Unless you are a master of the compound/complex sentence, avoid its use. The simpler your sentence structure, the easier it will be to understand the sentence.

Compare the following sentences and groups of sentences. Those that are simply written are far easier to read.

Wordy: The proliferation of paper and the many categories into which it would have to be separated, necessitated the invention of the paper clip.

Simple: The paper clip was invented to assemble scattered papers into neat groups.

Wordy: I was very excited to learn that my essay was the winning one and would have the capability of garnering an encomium in the competition that was planned under state auspices.

Simple: I was excited that my essay won and would be eligible for the state competition.

Read the following essay. It is wordy, awkward, and even unpleasant.

The world of advertising is very often described as a game of who can fool whom, and millions upon millions of dollars are spent trying to convince the unknowing masses, at least to the advertiser, to buy a product that they really don't actually need.

If that isn't enough, when a new product is introduced, at least five or ten copies from different companies will enter the supermarket shelves almost overnight, and to make matters worse, the more copies of products you see, the more likely the commercials to advertise those products begin to proliferate and almost seem the same.

For example, have you ever noticed how much alike the soft-drink commercials are? They all use music and show happy, smiling, healthy, active people. Commercials, even those which are generally well done, often seem to get so monotonous and confusing, you

can hardly tell a Coke commercial from
a Pepsi commercial. How are the consumers to make a choice when they are
bombarded every single time they turn
on their television or radio? How, on
the other hand, can advertisers hope
to gain a share in the marketplace if
they don't sink their product name
into the minds of the consumers?

Now read its revision. Notice how quickly you can skim
through it because it was edited so well.

In a game often described as "who
can fool whom," advertising agencies
spend millions of dollars trying to
convince the unknowing masses to buy a
product they actually don't need. To
compound the problem, companies load
supermarket shelves with "copycat"
products and then develop commercials—one much like the other—to
sell them.
   Have you ever noticed how similar
soft-drink commercials are? They all
use the same-sounding music and all
show smiling, active people having a
wonderful time. The commercials are
so monotonous and confusing, it's
nearly impossible to discern a Coke
from a Pepsi spot.
   The duplicity makes it impossible
for consumers to make a choice when
they are constantly bombarded by copycat commercials of copycat products. On the other hand, how can
advertisers strive to gain a healthy
share of the marketplace if they don't

plant their product's name in the consumers' minds?

CHOPPINESS

Conversely, sentences that are short and choppy are hard to read because the reader loses concentration when he or she must stop too often.
Read the first paragraph; then read the revision:

The shark is a fascinating animal.
It can be compared to a human being.
The reason is that both sharks and humans kill. But they do it for different reasons. The shark always kills to
eat. The human often kills to kill.
The motivations are different. Some
say it is because the shark has a small
brain. Its brain is geared only to
find prey. A human being has a more
highly evolved brain. This kind of
brain does more than find prey. The
human can read, think, laugh, and eat.
Yet, the human does kill. Why? If we
only knew the answer. But it is too
complicated.

The shark is a fascinating animal,
and although it swims in the sea, it
can be compared to another fascinating animal: the human being. Although
for different reasons and motivations, both these creatures kill. The
shark's motivation to kill is largely
controlled by its need to eat. Some
scientists believe this need is the
only driving force propelling the
shark. Because its brain is so small,
it only functions to detect prey. A

human being possesses a more highly evolved brain; he or she can read, think, laugh, and eat without having to kill. Yet, humans do kill. Why? Just as the human brain is so complicated, so are the answers as to why such a highly evolved creature would also kill just like a shark.

Obviously, the second paragraph is clearer and easier to read and holds the reader's interest because ideas flow smoothly from one sentence to the next.

IMAGERY

The metaphor and simile are not relegated to poetry. When used correctly in prose, they enhance the writing by creating pictures in the reader's mind. Note the differences:

Prosaic: Math frightened me.

Simile: Going to math class was like stepping into a dark closet where Steven Spielberg's most vicious gremlins lived.

Prosaic: Atlantic City lights up every night.

Metaphor: At night, Atlantic City makes her debut with the splendor of a fairy queen.

Prosaic: My chemistry teacher made things very easy to understand.

Simile: Like a pickax chipping away at a buried treasure, my chemistry teacher unearthed every mystery hidden in the chemical experiment.

Read the essay on pages 117 to 119 to see how, when used correctly, imagery can play an important part in written expression.

CLICHÉS

If you venture into the use of poetry in your essay, beware that you don't trap yourself into using clichés. Avoid expressions like "as thin as a rail," "as hungry as a horse," and "all the world's a stage." If you cannot create your own images, we suggest you use none at all.

See what happens in this first draft when the writer becomes entrenched in clichés:

The LaSalle Camp for the Performing Arts is nestled between two mountains at the foothills of the Adirondacks, a perfect place for culture and inspirational aspirations to be realized. I attended this camp for five of my formative years and had hoped beyond hope that they would accept me as a junior counselor in the theatrical division when I became fourteen and a half. I guess my pleading, cajoling, and persistence paid off because I received notification that I would be the junior counselor and I was happy as a lark. I would be going to LaSalle.

Anyway, camp was in full session when it was decided that the year-end play would be Once Upon A Mattress. I was thrilled beyond words because I had played Queen Agravain in my junior high school play at Menlo Park, and I knew the play so well that I felt sure that the audition would be like falling off a log and I would easily win the role. Well, you can just imagine my crestfallen face when it was announced in no uncertain terms that staff could not perform. Only campers were permitted to be in the show. I was green with envy. I would only be able to assist the director.

I just stamped my feet like a spoiled brat
and stewed in utter dismay, until I found
out that I had been selected to direct the
Agravain-Dauntless scenes all by myself.
From crestfallen to star-spangled rocket
glaring ecstasy was the resulting feeling
embued in me when I found out. Now I would
have the ultimate opportunity to direct two
aspiring, inexperienced actors to perform exactly what I envisioned and see it through to
the bitter end. You can't imagine the whoosh
of thrills I felt to have such monumental
control over two individuals who would
have to come to me for their instructions.

The night of nights arrived at last. I was
shaking like a leaf. All the hard work I had
done to see the two actors perform the way I
wanted them to would now be seen by everyone
at the camp who mattered and I would get the
credit.

Anyway, to make a long story short, the
two actors performed wonderfully, beautifully, artfully. I got the performance from
them I knew they had in them. They got the
applause, but in no uncertain terms, I received the ultimate reward. I guess that's
how the renowned Pee Wee Herman must have
felt when his great movie opened. What can I
say? It was all I had ever wanted and more,
so much more than mere words can ever express.

After removing all of the embarrassing clichés, this
student was able to make her final version have an entirely
new perspective. It is more focused, better directed, and
leads to a stronger, more impressive conclusion.

Being notified that I was accepted as a junior counselor at the LaSalle Camp for the Performing Arts was the culmination of a dream I had had for five years, since I was a camper there.

Camp was in full session and I was doing well, when I learned that the year-end play would be <u>Once Upon A Mattress</u>. That did it! I knew I was destined for stardom because I had played Queen Agravain in my junior high school play the year before. I felt as if I were leading a charmed existence. I had the job I had always dreamed of and now I was destined to play one of the leads in the year-end play. With this in mind, I auditioned and felt sure I had won the part.

It was one very long, disappointing day when I discovered the part was not mine. The charmed spell had been broken. My job was to assist the director. I was crestfallen. To rise so high and to sink so low in one day was unbearable, until I learned that I had been selected to direct the Agravain-Dauntless scenes myself. My first reaction was that this was merely a ''crumb'' from the director. But then I decided to make the most of the experience. Why not teach two inexperienced actors to perform exactly how I envisioned the part? After all, I really was a junior <u>director</u>, not junior <u>actress</u>. Maybe my charmed spell hadn't been broken after all.

After many hours of long rehearsals, my two actors were prepared to ''hit the boards.'' Opening night arrived and I couldn't stop myself from feeling the notorious butterflies in my stomach. Even

though I wouldn't be on stage, my ideas
would be, as reflected in my young actors.
And they performed beautifully. While they
bowed to tumultuous applause onstage, I did
the same backstage.

Though I never expected this outcome, it
was probably more rewarding than if I had
been given the part itself. I learned to accept a disappointment and turn it into a
valuable experience. In the future, as I
pursue an acting career, I will remember how
that summer at LaSalle prepared me to accept
the ups and downs inherent in this profession. If I could do it at fourteen and a
half, I can do it again and again!

POINT OF VIEW

The essay you write must be truthful, basically because
it's the honorable thing to do. But if you need a practical
reason, it's this: When you get to the interview and your
essay comes up in discussion, something that is not true
will come blazing through like a comet on a starless night—
and good-bye college! But telling a truth that will cast you
in a negative light is foolish.

In the essay below, the author describes her experiences working in a hospital gift shop. She chose the job
for the wrong reason. She disliked working in the shop
and was alienated by many of the people who frequented
it. But see for yourself:

I initially volunteered to work at Forth-
right Medical Center Gift Shop because I
thought it would be an easier and more
cheerful job than working around the hospital as a candy striper. I knew they were just
"dandified" go-fers in uniforms and I

didn't want to run around being nice and doing errands. At the gift shop, I could be in one place and help people make selections to help cheer up the patients they would be visiting.

Boy, was I wrong! The gift shop was actually the meeting place for many ambulatory elderly patients who wanted to purchase magazines and gum. I'll never understand why they wanted gum because they had no teeth. They were, for the most part, a grumpy lot. They managed their pennies as if these mere cents were millions of dollars and they were investing in gold mines instead of gumballs. For instance, they would badger me no end when the sales tax went up and they had to spend two cents more for a package of gum. They'd say, "It's the same five pieces. I don't have to support the state for my gum." They'd leave 25 cents and amble out with no sense of guilt, and I'd have to pay the difference out of my own money. They were real pains.

All I wanted to do was serve the nice people and help them select boxes of chocolate or floral arrangements. These people never argued with me about how much the presents cost. I felt I was making a real contribution in helping to get their friends and relatives better. That was fun. But for the most part, working with the old people was pure frustration. When I get older, I hope I'm never like that.

True, this essay is honest, but the writer appears uncaring. Although this may not be true, the author does not give the reader any evidence to the contrary.

She had two options. Either she should have limited her essay to the rewarding aspects of the job or she should have chosen some other experience to write about. Though her essay is fairly well written, we suspect the admissions committee would find it objectionable.

There is a lesson to be learned here. When choosing an essay topic, be certain what you say about yourself creates a positive image in the reader's mind. An admissions committee, no matter how impressed it may be with your credentials, will probably look askance at an essay that presents a student in an unfavorable light.

POMPOSITY

The following essay is about as verbose as an essay can be. The author is striving harder to impress the reader with his extensive command of English than with his ability to be a hardworking, responsible employee. Undoubtedly, the writer relied heavily on *Roget's Thesaurus*. But his reliance was so misdirected that he even substitutes "prevaricated" for "prevailed."

We cite this essay as an example of misguided bravura.

While Goldstein, Glipson, Slotnick, and Blum law firm may not have the patina of a Skadden—Arps, Guthrie, Rose, and Mudge, Polk, Waddel or Bacon Saxe, to be enabled to travail at the law firm in which my father, Sidney Glipson, was a senior partner for the summer was an exalting, yes, uplifting, and one of the most rewarding experiences of the modicum of years I had achieved within my lifetime. Obviously, it was not within the realm of my father's largess to offer me a position in which I might affect the outcome of a pro bono publico matter, but I

nevertheless had had the foresight to en-
gage myself in learning how to master the
word processor and therefore, it was not
without substantiation that the position of
junior word processor was acquired by me.

The exigencies of this position necessitated not just prosaic time, but a full com-
plement of unflinching stalwart patience.
For it stands to reason that in legal matters, the writing must of necessity be suc-
cinct and circumscribed. There was many a
prabble through which I had to wait, over
changes in just one paragraph involving a
litigious suit, the loss of which would have
meant thousands of dollars in the coffers of
our adversaries. Ah, but the noble lady jus-
tice always prevaricated. And even though
we would labor until the first glimmerings
of Eos, it was with a great deal of "amour
propre" that I would complete and deliver
the legal document.

Needless to say, the summer terminus came
upon us "ventre a terre," and it was with a
dull pang in the repository of my heart that
I had to cease functioning in this exceptional position and proceed into my next so-
journ in school. Perhaps I would learn some
precious gems of wisdom at Tremont High to
assist me in my quest for the grande entrée
into the hallowed halls of higher education. But they would never quite compare to
the inestimable education I received in the
law firm of Goldstein, Glipson, Slotnick,
Blum, and, one day (I pray), "and son," law
firm.

Rather than having submitted what is clearly a loath-
some piece of work, the author could have simply written:

Goldstein, Glipson, Slotnick, and Blum is a law firm in which my dad is a partner. Though it may not be as prestigious a firm as some, it was a rewarding experience to work there this past summer. Because I had mastered the word processor in high school, my dad was able to offer me a position as a junior word processor without feeling any guilt about me performing a "do-nothing" job.

I learned quickly that the writing of legal drafts involves many changes. Once I had completed the first draft, I was proud that I'd done a fine job. But no sooner did I finish congratulating myself than I had to revise that draft. Before the end of the day, I had processed nearly thirty revisions. I was near the end of my rope. But the attorneys weren't satisfied with the wording, and it wasn't until the thirty-fifth revision that agreement was reached.

On that first day I learned two important lessons. The first is in the matter of legal procedures where millions of dollars weigh in the outcome. The choice of words and the logic behind them is of primary importance. The case must be "airtight" and the attorneys who present it must be convinced that this is so. The second lesson is that if you happen to be a junior word processor in your father's law firm for the summer, patience is truly the only virtue.

At summer's end, I was sorry to leave. I'd made new friends and learned a great deal, some of which I expect can be applied as I continue my education in order to become an attorney. And if my dad's law firm is still around by the time I graduate, I wouldn't mind adding my name beside his.

This revised version shows a more mature and likeable individual. The person hasn't changed, but the direction and style of the essay have. And that's made all the difference.

In summation, probably the best advice we can give you at this point is a quotation from the seventeenth-century French writer Nicolas Boileau: "Whatever we conceive well, we express clearly."

SAMPLE ESSAYS

5

The essays that follow were authored by high school students from across the country. Certainly, they are not all perfectly written, but all have merit. Each allows us to get to know the author. You'll discover that no essay is boastful; no essay is synthetically modest. And no essay is a plea for acceptance.

We think you will be able to determine which are the weaker and which are the stronger. The comments that follow each essay attempt to explain both why they are effective and where they have shortcomings.

We cannot substantiate that the essay was the key reason why each student was accepted to college. There were other variables to be considered: grades, SAT scores, extracurricular activities, community service, personal qualities. We do know that each student was accepted to the college of his or her choice.

Topic: Evaluate a significant experience or achievement that has special meaning for you.

The day after graduation from junior high school, I saw Stuyvesant for the first time. I had come to the building to audition for the school's music program. I had been playing the flute for two years, and so I felt

Student taking the PSAT exam in New York City

that it certainly couldn't hurt to try out for Stuyvesant's music organization. What did I have to lose? If I were accepted, it would be fun. If I didn't make it, so what? Now I am in the program for the fourth year, a member of the band and the orchestra, and it has occurred to me that my tenure in the music program has had a much greater effect on me than that impressionable eighth-grader ever could have imagined.

Time was when I would turn on my Walkman on my way to school and listen to "top 40" songs by popular groups like Genesis, Mike and the Mechanics, and Heart. I tolerated the likes of Rodgers, Porter, Gershwin, and Sondheim, my parents' favorites, but I would literally tune out Brahms or Bach. Listening to a fugue was futile. But now, it seems, though I still enjoy listening to pop and rock music, I have discovered that classical music is infiltrating my listening repertory. I find my Walkman is now often replaced by my stereo filling the living room with 75 watts of Mozart, while Journey has taken a hiatus and Placido Domingo is slowly replacing Dire Straits. Even I am amazed!

Playing pieces in school like Wagner's Die Meistersinger and Beethoven's Fifth has taught me that there is room in my life for my favorite pop groups on one level and the heritage of hundreds of years of serious music on another. I have learned that it's equally as exciting to get swept up by the harmonies created by a synthesizer as it is by the harmonics in a Vivaldi strings passage.

I guess I owe my newly discovered enthusiasm to my music teacher, who scolded me
into scales, pounced on me to practice, re-
buked me to rehearse, who harrassed me with
affection and taunted me with tenderness. I
am not a candidate for the New York Philhar-
monic nor do I ever plan to be. But I am a
fledgling musician, grateful that my
teacher saw what talent I may have and con-
sented to nurture it. I am grateful that he
showed me there is as much pleasure in Von
Suppe as there is in Van Halen.

I even found myself convincing him to include "The Great Gates of Kiev" in an arrangement of highlights from Pictures at an
Exhibition the school band was playing. To
think that three years ago I didn't know
Pictures at an Exhibition from writing on a
bathroom wall.

Three years ago, I was trying to become
part of a music program that has now become a
part of me. Three years ago, I played flute.
Now I play music, and music plays a vital
role in my life.

This well-structured essay cleverly convinces the reader
that the author has indeed had a significant experience
with music. While the essay begins very simply, it ends
with a crescendo of poetic style as the author reveals how
music became more meaningful in his life. We believe
this kind of essay is one that will probably stand out among
the members of the admissions committee, not only because it reveals a unique writing style, but because it
reveals a unique person.

Topic: Tell us something about yourself that this application has not covered.

Did you know that one out of every four
people in the United States suffers from
some hearing loss?

How often have you actually thought about
it? I mean, really considered what it might
be like to be hard of hearing?

Exactly. Most people don't. It's the
"hidden handicap." You'd think that with
statistics like one-in-four, the public
would be aware of the hearing impaired, but
they're just not. How many deaf people wear
dark glasses, carry a white cane, or have a
gigantic dog with them to define their disa-
bility? None. They don't. We don't. Yes, I
have been hard of hearing for almost fourteen years, and I can tell you firsthand
that people don't know how to help the hearing-impaired.

After college, I'm planning to pursue
graduate work in the field of deaf studies,
possibly at the University of Boston. I want
to go into either the psychology of the deaf
or the teaching of the hearing-impaired. I
think it's extremely important to provide
the means for both cultures to join together
and be able to communicate with one another.
But I'd like to go about this in another way.
I want to incorporate the hearing into the
silent world, through awareness and through
sign language.

If students are required to take a foreign language, what better than sign language, the language of ideas? Or how about a
simple course in the manual alphabet? It's
really not difficult to learn. In fact, last
summer I worked as a junior counselor at a
day camp and I taught the manual alphabet to

a group of three—to—five—year—olds while we
sang our "ABC's." By the end of the camp
quite a few of them were singing along with
me! That's wonderful, isn't it? No, unfortunately it is not, because that will probably be the last time they ever see it.
I would love to go down in history as the
woman who brought signing language to the
American school system and to the world!
Am I a dreamer?
No. I am a doer. It may take a while, but I
have time. The world isn't going anywhere—
only I am!

This essay strikes a responsive chord among those
who are not aware what the world of the deaf is like. The
writer does it simply and clearly and offers an intelligent
solution for further understanding. Her determination to
teach signing to everyone is clearly evident, and her enthusiasm does not dim even when she admits that her
teaching the youngsters the manual alphabet was probably futile. Note, especially, her positive concluding sentence. You cannot help but smile.
This next essay, rather than describing an invention,
has a unique point of view. The author presents his acceptance speech at the prize-presentation ceremony.

Topic: You have just won a prize for your invention. Describe your invention and why you created it.

"I'm extremely gratified and happily
surprised to be accepting this prestigious
award from you, the members of the Couch Potato Society," I said as I stood at the
dais. The Couch Potato Society is one dedicated to the furtherance of TV watching to
any extreme. They had awarded me this year's

cash prize for my invention. In order to more fully acquaint you with my invention and why it was selected as the best, I've decided to present my acceptance speech as I delivered it that eventful evening.

"As I give this speech, some of you may be wondering, 'Why would I ever need a remote control _for_ my remote control?' Well, my fellow Couch Potatoes, I have some facts which may enlighten you: the average citizen with an income between $25,000 and $50,000 loses an average of 6–10 hours in a lifetime searching for his or her remote control. These numbers are bound to rise as TV watching, and especially remote-control TV watching, inevitably increase. I estimate that by the year 2036, that figure will be 6.4–10.3 hours. And for a Couch Potato, that number is raised to 7–11 hours.

"Some may look at those numbers and laugh, but wasted time is no laughing matter. An adult could watch up to twenty more Mary Tyler Moore reruns due to this invention, or an astounding two hundred more 30-second commercials, which I predict will increase by .361% if used by half of all American remote-control-TV users. Think of the boost this would give our economy.

"Before concluding this acceptance speech, I would like to draw attention to the fine inventions of the runners-up, who, in their noble efforts to further TV watching everywhere, had as good a chance of winning as I: J.P. Pickle for his remote-control beer-can opener and Henry P. Jones with his remote-control remote-control remote-control.

"In conclusion, I would like to plainly state that TV and its first cousin, the VCR, are the tools that will lead America to its future stagnation! I hope that my humble invention will further that cause. I thank you."

The writer is very daring in attempting to present himself to the admissions committee with an essay that is unusual in its style and droll in its point of view. Although the essay does merit attention, it could be the kind of attention that is more of a hindrance than a help, depending on the makeup of a particular admissions committee at a particular school.

Topic: Please comment on the book or motion picture you recommended most enthusiastically to your friends during the last year.

The whole world is plagued by an epidemic that has been caused by humankind itself, an epidemic created by nuclear research. Even though nuclear research has brought about some positive results, nuclear weapons, if used, promise dire consequences. Other examples of modern progress, like Chernobyl and Three Mile Island, have already brought forth more negative than positive ends. It is possible that this modern progress is a step backward for humankind. Ray Bradbury illustrated this point in his story "There Will Come Soft Rains," from The Martian Chronicles, before anyone ever heard of Reagan's Strategic Defense Initiative.

We must understand that the world today is preoccupied with self-protection. People of different nationalities fear and hate each other because they are not able to understand one another's values or cultures. It seems to me that we live "like children in a dying forest, alone, alone," instead of taking the time to look at our similarities rather than our differences. We fear that certain people are a threat to our well-being and therefore we build weapons to protect ourselves from these "barbarians."

The superpowers have built tons of nuclear weapons which have given them the ability to destroy the world several times over. In this respect, the arms race can have no victor. Bradbury makes this point by describing the result of nuclear devastation: "The house stood alone in a city of rubble and ashes. This was one house left standing. At night the ruined city gave off a radioactive glow that could be seen for miles." He shows us that the world's paranoia can only lead to complete destruction. This threat is a direct consequence of our so-called "progress."

Bradbury reinforces my belief that modern progress will cause more harm than good. The people in the story had only one purpose in life—to exist. The house was the symbol of the society since it was the only thing left standing. The fact that the house was able to survive without its inhabitants showed that this fully automated world was self-sufficient and to exist did not need people. Consequently, the people of that society became careless and lazy. The house took care of everything: "Wall panels flipped open and copper scrap rats flashed swiftly out. The offending dust, hair, or paper, seized in miniature steel jaws, was raced back to the burrows. " All responsibility was given to the house. The people seemed to have sacrificed their humanity for their comfort.

The most significant consequence of their dependence on machines, however, was that they became mindless. The house told them how to conduct their daily lives: "It repeated the date three times for memory's sake. 'Today is Mr. Featherstone's birthday. Today is the anniversary of Titila's marriage. Insurance is payable as are the water, gas, and light bills.'" It told them what to wear. The house even usurped their imagination, as illustrated by the description of the nursery with its mechanical animals. The inhabitants expressed no preferences. They ate what they were given and slept when they were told to. They had become the machines of their machines. In short, I surmised that Bradbury's message is that our reliance on machines will make us useless, careless, and mindless. Not a very positive message for someone who'd like to increase his depth of learning!

Undoubtedly, progress sometimes causes more problems than it is worth. Our military program is an example of this. We are trying to deploy weapons in space because we are not satisfied with the predicament with which we are already faced. I think the use of nuclear energy has created toxic wastes which endanger our land and health because we cannot properly dispose of the wastes. And yet we continue to rely on automation by accepting it as flawless. Just a few years ago, the United States was warned of a nuclear attack that turned out to be false. Bradbury might say that this was an example of "mechanical paranoia." In "There Will Come Soft Rains" the house's paranoia can only be viewed as a reflection of the society's paranoia: "How carefully it had inquired, 'Who goes there? What's the password?' and getting no answer from lonely foxes and whining cats, it has shut up its windows and drawn shades in an old-maidenly preoccupation with self-protection which bordered on a mechanical paranoia."

The people in the story thought that their machines were so perfect that they did not even fear putting nuclear weapons in the hands of the machines and in so doing put the fate of the world in the hands of machines. Consequently, they were annihilated in "one titanic instant," just as the house was.

Modern progress does have its benefits. However, I believe this progress is coming too quickly for us to handle. Furthermore, if all the advantages of modern progress can be wiped out by nuclear weapons, then is any of it worth it?

This student cleverly interjects his point of view about nuclear weapons through his review of Ray Bradbury's work. By citing intelligent examples of how the science fiction of Ray Bradbury relates to our lives now, the student convinces the reader of his enthusiasm for the author and his concern about the world's future. The essay, however, could be edited some by citing fewer examples.

Here's quite a different slant on the same essay topic. We think it's charming.

Fourteen years ago, when my brother Steve was born, it was reported that I made such statements as: "I'd rather have a puppy," and "Let's put him in the mailbox." My view about having a sibling has since changed as I've grown more empathetic.

Eight months ago, my mother gave birth to my youngest brother. This time, I'm enjoying it. I've reshelved my Harlequin Romances and have become a devotee of Dr. Spock. No, not the Spock with the pointy ears. It's the Benjamin Spock with points of view about rearing children that interest me because I see my brother develop just the way Dr. Spock says he will.

Just the other day, I was reading the chapter about when the baby actually acknowledges one person as different from another. My mother and I tried an experiment. She stood on one side of my brother's crib while I stood on the other. I called, "Chuckie!" in my typical baby-talk tone. Chuck turned to me, smiled, and gurgled. I beamed! He recognized me. Dr. Spock was correct.

Next, my mother called to him. He turned, smiled, and reached out to her. My beaming slowly faded. Shelley was Shelley, but Mom was Mom. He really knew the difference.

Though I was a bit disappointed, I received, nonetheless, my first lesson in the gospel according to Spock—all babies' attention is first drawn to their mothers. It was as it should have been and nobody knows their baby business better than he.

Who would believe that I, a normal seventeen-year-old, ready to enter college, would be reading Dr. Spock? For that matter, who would have thought that my mother would be having a baby at her age? Mother and son (and daughter) are doing fine. Thanks, Doc.

Topic: Which of your talents or interests would you like to develop further during your college years? Explain fully.

The first contact I had with industrial and labor relations was through my father. He was graduated from the New York State School of Industrial Relations at Cornell University and is currently working in personnel management. After many years of dinnertime discussions about labor relations, I have developed a keen interest in the area. My dad was able to arrange for me to speak with people who work in different aspects of the field, and through them my knowledge has grown appreciably.

I met with a gentleman who worked with the United Mine Workers Union and is presently employed as a mediator with the Federal Mediation and Conciliation Service. He spoke of the challenge of trying to organize new union locals and revitalizing old ones. Mr. Swanson then went on to explain his role as a mediator. It is his job to find a middle ground between labor and management. He must work with both parties by explaining the demands of each group to the other. I learned it is important that the mediator understand both their goals and, in addition, which areas are of primary importance. The mediator must be able to convince both sides to concede that reaching an agreement involves compromises by both parties.

At a session of the American Arbitration
Association between a Teamsters Union local
and the Meadowbrook Dairy, I followed a case
that concerned the loss of a sum of money.
However, the employee involved was not
charged with theft because both parties
felt that there was negligence on the part
of many people. The arbitration was held to
determine how much money the employee would
pay back to the dairy. The atmosphere was
quite congenial and resulted in the union
and the management resolving the problem
without the arbitrator rendering a decision. There were constant deliberations as
various groups of men stepped outside the
arbitration room in an attempt to reach a
congenial agreement. While these men were
locked in intense discussion, the remaining
men chatted casually as if they were at the
local club. Such a friendly spirit, I was
informed, was not present in most arbitra-
tions. It was the nature of the case that allowed for this type of atmosphere. If the
employee were to be discharged, there certainly would have been far more animosity.

Another aspect of the labor relations
field is labor law. A well-respected labor
attorney explained that it was his job to
inform his clients of what they can legally
do about a labor issue. He also represents
his clients at hearings, preparation for
which takes a great deal of his time, since
so many new aspects of labor inequities have
recently surfaced. The stress today is on
challenging discrimination in labor based
on sex, race, or age, areas previously ignored in the courts.

These experiences have helped me to further my knowledge of the field of industrial and labor relations. I hope to pursue this career, possibly as a mediator or an attorney. It seems to me that serving as a mediator or attorney would be a rewarding responsibility. Certainly, the example my father sets reinforces this point of view.

Though this essay is less dramatic than most of the others, it does what it is supposed to do. The writer demonstrates his interest in labor relations by citing several instances in which he has had firsthand knowledge. It is significant that he has had the initiative to attend actual mediating sessions and as an observer learned the roles each member had to play. He clearly expresses what he has learned and how this knowledge has influenced his career choice.

Topic: What does "success" mean to you? Explain how it reflects your lifestyle.

Success, to me, is to enjoy life and use my own individual talents and creativity as fully as possible. This creativity is a blend of energy and curiosity. The greatest artists of history are united by the powerful characteristic of energy. They use their lives to experience as much as they possibly can. Everything becomes a part of the rhythm of life—beauty, pain, hate, loneliness, love. And living with a passionate intensity is what inspires creative genius.

Every person must constantly choose to actively taste every morsel of feeling that life has to offer. Donald Peattie, in

<u>An Almanac for Moderns</u>, defines the atti-
tude: "Life is an adventure in experience,
and when you are no longer greedy for the
last drop of it, it means no more than you
have set your face . . . to the day when you
shall depart. . . ."
  <u>Carpe diem.</u> In Latin, "seize the day."
This is a theme I discovered in studying the
seventeenth-century English cavalier
poets. It's important to realize that this
intense mindset is a conscious action, to
feel. It is more than sensitivity. Pure sensitivity is a reaction, while living intensely is an action.
  I think that living with such raw vigor
results in a widening flood of creative energy flowing through the individual. However, life cannot be all emotion; a balance
must exist between experience and obliga-
tion. Then, once a harmonious equilibrium
has been reached, the energy can be har-
nessed and channeled into the process of
creativity. So the energy is constantly
moving in a cycle: it is first used to live
life, and then reappears as creative energy. Energy is the lifeblood of creativity.
  The life of Henry David Thoreau proves to
me the value of this emotional intensity.
The two years he spent at Walden Pond were no
whirlwind of social or cultural activity,
but Thoreau immersed himself in the natural
setting. Life itself excited him, among the
grass, animals, sky, and water. And his
works reflect the brilliance which sprang
from his mind in that environment.
  I found another example of this lifestyle
in David Amram, a widely recognized contem-

porary composer and musician. I watched him
onstage, directing his own works, flying
around, laughing, conducting, performing,
bringing the audience to a clapping, de-
lighted frenzy. Amram is obviously both
happy and fulfilled. He travels extensively
and lives on a tight schedule; he is fast-
paced, yet remains thoughtful and produc-
tive. He has achieved his balance, a balance
that I, too, want to achieve.

History is rich with such examples—Van
Gogh, Mozart, Dickinson, Bernstein—all
have lived with a desperate fervor, and
their maniacal intensity, expressed so elo-
quently in their art, is what has immortal-
ized them.

I want to follow such examples in leading
my own life. Living it with energy is extremely important to me. I want to enjoy
everything as much as possible. And I hope
that if I use my time fully and experience as
much as I can, I'll begin to formulate some
ideas about people and the world, and I'll
have the creative energy to express them
clearly, originally, and productively.

The whole wide world is out there, pound-
ing with emotions and all kinds of ideas and
experiences I've never even thought of before. Even my life here and now, in high
school, is a valuable experience, and I'm
trying to live it fully and use my time to
wring out every drop of feeling I can. "You
only live once," and there's no end to the
possibilities this life holds for development and exploration.

This student has connected the lives of artistic ge-
niuses to the idea of "success" and goes one step fur-

ther—she relates the artists and their energies to her own life and goals she has set for herself.

The essay reflects the writer's exuberance, intelligence, and passionate zest for living while she writes with depth, clarity, and sensitivity. She could eliminate one or two examples to make the essay crisper.

Topic: Suppose you had the opportunity to spend a day with anyone. With whom would it be and how would you spend your time?

I thought this question out thoroughly. Many people came to mind: Emerson, Harry Chapin, my ancestors, Xavier Cugat (just to find out where he got his name), even Adam and Eve. I had two great questions for them. One, what was Earth like in its undisturbed, virgin state? And two, did they have belly buttons? (Think about that.)

But I guess if I could spend an evening with anyone who ever lived, have a one-on-one conversation with any one great figure, or even any regular Joe, in all of history, I would want to spend an evening with God.

Seriously, you'd have to be crazy (or an atheist) not to. The evening would answer all of my questions about God. What does he look like? ("Does he look anything like George Burns?" falls into this category.) What kind of person is God, anyway? Is he the kind of guy you could put your arm around, chuck under the chin, and have a beer with?

I have to admit, however, that I don't think I'd be a very good host/guest, because I have the feeling that I would just bombard him with question after question. How did the universe begin? Is there a heaven? Is

Christ really the Messiah? Where is Jimmy Hoffa? How did you pull off the '69 Mets? Is there a Santa Claus? Is my hair all right? And so on.

Now, some people (actually many people) would find this essay offensive and blasphemous. They would exclaim, "How can you talk about the Lord in such a flip, sardonic tone? How dare you attempt to bring the Lord onto your level? How dare you refer to Him as 'he' and 'him,' as if he were common?" Well, I guess I should start my explanation by saying that I am Jewish, but I consider myself more a member of the Jewish culture than of the Jewish religion. You see, I believe that everyone should have his or her own, personal relationship with God, a relationship that should not be influenced by others. That's why I feel that "organized religion" is kind of wrong.

In organized prayer services, we are told what to pray, and actually told the exact words for how to pray it. In a Jewish service, we are to pray in a foreign language that the uneducated cannot even read, much less pronounce. I have been told that we pray in Hebrew because it is the holy language, and the language that God understands. I would ask if God understood English and be told that he did. When I would ask why we don't pray in English, the subject would be changed. I always liked the "silent prayer" part of the service best, because then I could speak to God the way I wanted to. I didn't have to talk to him in a language that I didn't understand. That's how I speak to God today. I talk to him as if he were a friend of mine, because that's how I feel most comfortable.

I'd like to know exactly how he feels about organized religion and about the people who are making a mockery of not just religion, but of God himself. What is his stand on the Hare Krishnas, Reverend Moon, Shagwan Shree Rajneesh, the Jonestown Kool-Aid cult, and other such groups? And what does he think about Jerry Falwell trying to impose his definition of what is right on the American people? The saying "We're all God's children" could be called into question before the evening was over.

All in all, I suspect that God is quite a fascinating guy.

This essay presents a strong point of view about religion. Although it appears as if the writer's tone is a bit too arrogant initially, we can detect a more reasonable point of view as the essay continues.

Its success, then, is because of its arrogance. The author "dares" to question and because she does and succeeds, she reveals how sophisticated her philosophy is. Her style is witty, clever, and engrossing. Nevertheless, the initial paragraph belies the depth of her thinking, and the point she makes, however strong it may be, could have been made without the opening paragraph and sooner.

Here is another treatment of the same essay topic in an entirely different style.

If I had the opportunity to spend an evening with someone of my choice, I would select the late actor James Dean. I envision him sitting in the last row of Radio City Music Hall, slumped in a chair, with a charac-

teristic scowl on his face. I am on stage
alone. A spotlight follows me. The rest of
the hall is in darkness. The following is
what I would like him to hear:
There are thirteen pictures of a man on my
wall. And they're of you, at different
stages of your life and career. I am not the
only one who views you as a cult hero or who
has seen your three films countless times.
Only three films in an entire lifetime! What
a waste! Some Hollywood stars turn out three
films a year.

Teenagers today need someone they can
idolize and model themselves after. It
makes things easier for them, gives them
fewer choices to contend with. There are so
many different ways to grow up, so many
paths to take. Many have tried to follow
your path. You were extremely talented and
popular, but you allowed your life to fall
apart, leading to your death. What kind of
model is that for today's youth?

I may have photos of you on my wall, but
at least I know what I am looking at. And
that is someone who, despite talent, drive,
public acclaim, and accomplishments, could
not make a real success of his life. True, I
have never made a movie, I have never been
involved in the Hollywood scene, and I have
never been subjected to the pressures you
have known. But I have found, in my own experiences, that life in the theatre can be de-
manding, exhausting, and lonely. People
only love you when you show them what they
want to see. You get two minutes of applause
or a good review. But after the production
is over, the costumes put away, the makeup

removed, you are left with only the memory.
You play your part for them and they praise
you. But what about when you play yourself?

I spent two summers studying intensely at
the Berkshire Ensemble for Theatre Arts. We
worked for over ten hours a day for five
weeks on a major production. After expend-
ing so much energy on four performances and
expecting the "limelight" for a short
time, I was faced all too soon with the end.
I worked very hard to remember the praise
and the feelings of accomplishment long
after the applause stopped. Not an easy
thing to do. But it is a critical thing. You
really are your own audience. If you can't
applaud yourself, you can't expect others
to make up for it.

Another summer program I was involved in,
the Narcotics Summer Counseling program,
exposed me to the problems of teenage alco-
holism and drug abuse. Students in this program were disillusioned, lonely, and
frightened, yet they knew enough to reach
out. By helping these young people estab-
lish healthy relationships with each other,
we aided them in rebuilding their self-confidence. The program showed them that they
had to rely on their inner strength and re-
sources rather than lead false, destruc-
tive, materialistic lives.

All over the country, people my age are
giving in to pressures and states of depres-
sion, and losing themselves by using dan-
gerous substances. They are trying to es-
cape—just as you were. Just as you did the
day you wrecked yourself on your motorcy-
cle. Reckless living solves very little.

Young people who are confused and in pain
need to learn how to overcome their problems
and build positive lives for themselves. A
true hero is one who learns from his or her
difficulties and reaches goals in spite of
them.

Yes, we are just as frightened for the future of America as you were in the fifties.
And yes, we are just as vulnerable to the influences of alcohol, if not more so now. It
is not your fault that you lived in a confused society, but it is your fault for al-
lowing your anger to corrupt your life. Give
us someone we can be proud to look up to,
give us a model of strength and endurance.
We are tired of those who "could have been."
It is time to celebrate those who survive,
not those who surrender.

The author is obviously intelligent and sensitive to the
needs of her peer group. She demonstrates her commit-
ment to helping others by citing her involvement in a summer narcotics counseling program. In addition, she discusses her dedication to the theatre ensemble and in
doing so, presents herself in a sophisticated manner. She
reveals her readiness to accept responsibilities through
her dedication to both summer positions. And she shows
she learned more about herself through these experiences. However, we believe she would have made a
stronger impression had she written in a more positive
tone, reflecting less anger and dismay.

Topic: Select your favorite quotation, or one that holds
special importance to you, and comment upon its significance.

A quotation that holds special importance for me is one that was said in 1848 by

Elizabeth Cady Stanton: "We hold these truths to be self-evident, that all men <u>and women</u> are created equal."

What a pity that Ms. Stanton isn't alive today to see how far women have come in what is still a male-dominated world. To be sure, women have gained the vote, women hold public office, women hold executive positions, and many even earn equal pay for equal work. However, those women who run for public office often spend more time defending themselves as women than telling what they have to offer as public servants. Women who have become executives—and there are very few—have spent more time proving themselves equal to or better than men vying for the same position than they have proving themselves worthy of the executive title.

Women have to defend not only their skill, but their ability to overcome perceived "female weaknesses." So many men in my family and so many of their male friends are advocates of these weaknesses. They still believe that women belong in the kitchen, barefoot and pregnant every year. Even at home, I am constantly trying to explain that I will not become a housewife because it is my destiny. If I marry, have children, and stay at home, it will be because I choose to, not because I am supposed to.

I am going to college to be educated so that I may compete on my own merits, to reach my own goals, to prove myself as the best in whatever profession I enter. If I marry, my marriage will be one based on equality. My career will be equally as important to my husband as his will be to me. The responsibility of rearing our children will be shared equitably. And our children will grow to understand that their lives will offer them choices, not directives.

What Ms. Stanton said was only a beginning. She was concerned that men and women were created equal. Today's concern is beyond that basic concept; it has become a desire, if not a demand, for equality throughout life. How pleased Ms. Stanton would be that her ideas have come so far. I wonder if she would be unhappy because they have not come far enough.

Clearly, this is a well-structured, intelligently written essay. The author has cited a quote that substantially influences every aspect of her life, now and for the future. It is a strong, positive statement and commands respect.

Here's a variation on the same essay topic, but treated very differently.

Adelaide Pinkerton was my very first teacher at Sun Lakes Elementary School. She was also my mother's first teacher and my older brother's first teacher. By the time it was my time to enter kindergarten, Mrs. Pinkerton had already taught generations of Kingston residents how to build with blocks, play games, and learn to count to ten. But at my first sight of this gray-haired, wizened old lady, I ran away. I had heard all the stories about how cheerful she was and how she loved her children, and I expected her to be young and pretty like my mom. I had no concept of time. Even Mr. Baxter, who owned the town drugstore and had white hair, remembered Mrs. Pinkerton when he went to school. I just never bothered to put the pieces together. But I became adjusted, and like all of her students, I grew to love her.

It wasn't until I graduated from elementary school that I realized that Mrs. Pinkerton had become one of the most important persons in my life. I asked her to sign my graduation album. As I waited in line for the others before me, it seemed to me as if she was laboring over every entry in their albums. But when it was my turn, she completed her remarks in record time. I was dismayed. I expected her to write an epistle to me since she had been a witness to my progress through all my elementary grades. She was there when I won the Spelling Bee, became captain of the basketball team, and became president of the Student Organization in the eighth grade.

With much trepidation, I opened the album to the page I had selected especially for her. Her entry read, "Little Cindy, DO IT! Adelaide Pinkerton." I was upset for days at the paucity of words and had no idea how much those words would mean to me as I began my high school years.

Mrs. Pinkerton's two words commanded me not to be afraid. She magically gave me the courage to conquer tasks I thought were difficult in high school, at home, and at work. It seemed that every time an onerous task was set before me, I'd put it aside if I had little confidence in accomplishing it successfully. For instance, although I am an excellent English student, I have never found science easy. I was placed in an honors chemistry class, and my gut feeling was that I didn't belong with my "genius" classmates. I didn't give myself any option except to abhor the predicament and therefore blur any likelihood of comprehension. I failed my first test. I brought my paper home and sobbed to my father, "I'm just dumb. There's no other explanation." My father would tell me to have patience and then reassure me that I wasn't dumb. Then, like magic, I would see those two words in my mind's eye and hear Mrs. Pinkerton echo them, "DO IT!" It was the catalyst I needed to put aside my fears and prejudices and tackle the subject. I worked diligently trying to understand the language of molecules. When I finally mastered and became glib in that subject area, I was pleased, but I knew Mrs. Pinkerton would have been even more pleased.

Most anyone can cite a quotation that has been meaningful at one time or another. But Mrs. Pinkerton's advice to me has been meaningful even as I am composing this essay. I expect it's ingrained in me, and that throughout the years of my higher education, when I finally decide what it is I want to do, I'll just go ahead and "DO IT!" and remember Mrs. Pinkerton.

In format, content, and style, this essay is superior. The author delays telling us what the quotation actually is by setting the scene to draw us in. The introductory two paragraphs tell us about the author and how she came to know the quotation. She then goes on to discuss how the statement remained with her throughout her school

years. Finally, she returns to discussing her teacher—a
full turn back to the introduction. We feel that this author
knows how to write a winning essay.

Topic: Indicate a person who has had a significant influence on you, and describe that influence.

Suh Chong Kang is the grandmaster of the
Tae Kwan Do karate camp and school in Brooklyn. Mr. Kang is the highest ranking instructor in both karate and Tae Kwan Do in
the world, is a tenth-dan (degree) black
belt, and has been training for 55 years.
Let me explain that Tae Kwon Do is a modernized version of an ancient form of Korean
unarmed combat, as are karate and judo (Japanese and Filipino styles of unarmed combat). But it is more than just kicks,
thrusts, and punches, and more than developing agility, balance, and coordination.
It is a way of disciplining the mind, a way
of getting in touch with one's spiritual
self.

Grandmaster Kang is 67 years old and
moves like a man of 20. When he walks into
the Do Jang (literally translated: place to
learn the way of life), my eyes, as well as
the eyes of the other students, turn toward
him, and we all bow in respect. He has earned
that respect. He seems not to be intimidated
by anyone or anything. He teaches that anything is possible if one puts his mind and
heart and soul into it, regardless of one's
sex, age, or race. He seems to be saying,
"You can unlock any door, only if you have
the right key." His eyes are kind, and he
talks quietly so that every mouth must be
closed and every ear opened to hear.

Grandmaster Kang takes the time to help any student who may have a problem with a certain move or kick. He never criticizes harshly or would allow anyone to feel foolish in front of other students. He has taught me to control my mind and body and, without using words, to expect respect only if I earn it. I admire the Grandmaster, and because of him, I am working to achieve the kind of self-confidence and inner strength he emanates. A perfect example of this achievement is his three sons, whom he has taught and who teach with him. Their resemblance to their father is uncanny, for they reflect that same kind of aura. Even though I have a long way to go, I hope someday that, like his sons, I will be a reflection of Grandmaster Suh Chong Kang.

In this essay, the student has demonstrated how the person has had an effect on his life and on his future goals. Its attributes are that it is artfully written, concise, descriptive, and reveals the admiration the writer has for his teacher.

Topic: Discuss some issue of personal, local, or national concern and its importance to you.

At night, Atlantic City makes her debut with the splendor of a fairy queen. She is radiant; her bright flashing lights lure men to her casino palaces. They spend millions so that they may gaze at her beauty. However, when dawn breaks, her veil falls. Her ugliness is revealed and men flee in horror. Her facade deceives only strangers, for her loyal subjects see her at all times and live under her constant rule.

As one of Atlantic City's subjects, I, too, see through her veil. Under her reign, we were promised just rule. She pledged to insure urban renewal, prosperity for merchants, and aid to her loyal subjects.

Her boardwalk glitters but her avenue cries. The casino queen has built great palaces for her own benefit and has not done anything to better the rest of the kingdom. The littered streets are lined with dilapidated buildings. They stand like matches ready to be ignited. The squalor is apparent not only in the streets but also in the air. The thick soot from caravans of buses pollute our once crisp ocean air.

The queen promised that she would attract buyers to the marketplace so that all merchants may partake of her wealth. Again she deceived us. Her lavish palaces lure men and distract them from the merchant on the avenue. The queen not only steals trade from small businesses but also collects exorbitant taxes from them. Merchants must pay high property taxes and high utility bills.

The queen's greatest injustice is her ungrateful treatment of her loyal subjects. When she needed the support of senior citizens, she vowed to help them. Yet now, she evicts them from their homes. She also pledged to bring benefits to others as well, but those benefits evolved into detriments. Her gambling palaces have brought drug trafficking, prostitution, and "gambling fever." This "fever" has caused many people to lose their homes and businesses. It affects not only adults but also students who, illegally, can be found in the casinos during the school day. The queen's influence has also discouraged them from pursuing higher education. They would rather perform mindless tasks for the queen in her palaces than labor to enrich themselves.

I tell this tale of our reigning queen so that men may not be dazzled by her feigned appearance. They must look deeper into her eyes to find her true character, her inner benevolence, and help her see the extent of her realm. Once she recognizes what they need and sees fit to help her subjects, she will indeed reign supreme. As her loyal subject, I will be among those courageous enough in their convictions to help broaden her horizons.

The personification of Atlantic City as a woman of splendor makes this unusual essay extremely effective. Rather than travel a prosaic course, the author chooses the harder route—poetic. And poetic it is. Through the vivid imagery, we are confronted with the perils of the author's home city and his concern for its future. He concludes by indicating what his hopes are for Atlantic City and how he will participate in making them a reality.

The following is an essay about a national problem, treated in a personal manner. We think it's an excellent piece of work.

As an eighteen-year-old high school senior, I'm aware of the myriad of problems besetting our nation and the world at large. Each one of them, from nuclear holocaust to the collapse of the world's economy, are areas I could address. I've studied economics and world banking at Elmira High School, and I've participated in group protests against nuclear war. Though both issues concern me in general, there is one issue that concerns me in particular. What is it? People still are not aware of the problems of the aging, specifically those suffering from Alzheimer's disease.

I grew up in one of the last vestiges of the extended family. My grandfather and grandmother lived with my two sisters, my brother, my parents, and me ever since my grandfather retired from his job as a New York City firefighter. My parents did not want them to stay in New York, and they finally moved to Elmira when my mom gave birth to her last child, my younger sister, now thirteen. It seemed a natural, as far as my parents were concerned. But my grandmother didn't want to give up her friends, nor did she want to be my mother's built-in babysitter. Grandma didn't want to owe anything to anybody. But my grandfather convinced her that the offer was genuine and that they could get more leverage from his pension and social security incomes because it was less expensive to live in Elmira. To be fair, my dad did build an extension apartment to our house so that Grandma and Grandpa had their own privacy. And Grandpa insisted on paying for it.

What surprised me was my grandmother's reaction to moving in. She was not herself. She virtually ignored my great marks at school, while they were greeted with exaltations by the rest of my family. And to think she was the one who always sent me five dollars when I read her my report card.

Then one day, she met a group of women at the library, and it seemed as if her personality changed overnight. She had friends.

She became involved in many civic organizations and often entertained at home with my grandfather proudly supporting her. By the time I was in high school, things had settled down to a very happy, well-adjusted routine. Grandma was the person who actually involved me in marches against nuclear armaments. Grandma could discuss my essays and themes with me and offer constructive criticism. She was always there.

But two years ago, Grandpa died. It was a brief illness, but it devastated us. Most of all, it affected my grandmother. Until then, I'd not realized what a devoted pair they were, and how much of her life was intertwined with his. Now Grandma found she was spending most of her time alone, and my sisters, my brother, and I were spending time hoping the Grandma we knew and dearly loved would return to us. During the next six months, she would not leave the house. Her most lucid moments, when we could see traces of her old self, were when she would talk about Grandpa—how smart, courageous, and handsome he was. She told us how they worked together to build an enviable relationship, how he loved his child and treasured his grandchildren. Then the smile would disappear and she'd sob grievously. There was nothing we could do for her. We sought help from a family counselor who advised us that with time this would pass and that she would not respond to our demands to end her grieving period until she was ready.

But she never seemed to be ready. Soon Grandma didn't talk at all. And when she did speak, her words were garbled. She'd forget our names. She forgot where the refrigerator was when she offered us some fruit as she usually did after school was out.

It was my younger sister who first mentioned these strange occurrences to my mom and dad. But they'd known about it already. They knew Grandma was suffering from Alzheimer's disease and that the first signs had appeared two years ago. Since Grandpa had always been there to cover for her simple mistakes, we just never noticed.

I'd heard about Alzheimer's and always felt that was one of the hazards of an increasingly greater life-span we Americans were beginning to enjoy. It occurred to me that this was really no way for an older citizen who appeared healthy, and had no financial worries, to live out the rest of her life. Because I wanted so much to see my grandmother become better, I joined the local chapter of the Alzheimer's Disease Foundation. It became an excellent source of help, comfort, and information. I realized we weren't the only family stricken in Elmira and that the problem was of nationwide proportions. But because it wasn't yet considered a catastrophic illness, there was no federal help available. Each time I sought another avenue of help, I was rebuffed.

My goal for the future is very focused now. I want to help to find a cure for Alzheimer's disease, which is destroying the lives of too many people in America. And though federal funds to be spent on finding a cure may be further cut because the economy is sluggish, I still believe I can contribute something to the generation who helped to mold me and my parents.

To me, the "graying of America" is not all it was cracked up to be. That Americans live longer is good, but they should be able to enjoy their longevity in better health. That is why I seek admittance to Tufts University, where I know the science department is terrific, and Tufts is the recipient of several research grants. Nothing would give me greater pleasure than to contribute to a better lifestyle for older Americans. Perhaps it may be too late for my grandma, but my research may help my mom and dad and eventually may help me as well as I intend to grow old and gray, but with grace and dignity.

Though you were advised that unless qualified, you should steer clear of issues of national concern, when you make that issue one of your own concern, the essay becomes compelling for the reader. A basic lesson in writing is: write what you know. Clearly, the author knew the situation, knew of its national implications, and concludes by personalizing this national problem through citing it as the basis of her career goals.

*Driscoll University Center Bridge,
University of Denver, Colorado*

CONCLUSION

You've just completed an arduous task by writing what you believe presents you to the admissions committee of the college of your choice in the best possible light. In taking control of this entire process, you've also learned more about yourself so that you were able to show the college why you are unique and why you are a worthy candidate to join its freshman class.

You were challenged and you met that challenge admirably. Now write or type a scrap copy of the essay, review it, revise it, and show it to your parents and teachers for criticism. Then take a day off to rest.

Once you are refreshed, review it once more, then prepare the final draft on the original application. Make a photocopy, which you will file for yourself. Address the envelope properly; apply the correct postage. Slip in the original and send it by registered mail. You've done all that you can. Relax. Now the college takes control.

We sincerely wish you good luck. You've earned it.

INDEX